JENNI CALDER WAS born in Chicago, educated in the United States and England, and has lived in or near Edinburgh since 1971. After several years of part-time teaching and freelance writing, including three years in Kenya, she worked at the National Museums of Scotland from 1978 to 2001 successively as education officer, Head of Publications, script editor for the Museum of Scotland, and latterly as Head of Museum of Scotland International. In the latter capacity her main interest was in emigration and the Scottish diaspora. She has written and lectured widely on Scottish, English and American literary and historical subjects, and writes fiction and poetry as Jenni Daiches. She has two daughters, a son and a dog.

By the same author:

Chronicles of Conscience: A Study of Arthur Koestler and George Orwell, Secker and Warburg, 1968
Scott (with Angus Calder), Evans, 1969
There Must be a Lone Ranger: The Myth and Reality of the American West, Hamish Hamilton, 1974
Women and Marriage in Victorian Fiction, Thames and Hudson, 1976
Brave New World and Nineteen Eighty-Four, Edward Arnold, 1976
Heroes, from Byron to Guevara, Hamish Hamilton, 1977
The Victorian Home, Batsford, 1977
The Victorian and Edwardian Home in Old Photographs, Batsford, 1979
RLS: A Life Study, Hamish Hamilton, 1980
The Enterprising Scot (ed, with contributions), National Museums of Scotland, 1986
Animal Farm and Nineteen Eighty-Four, Open University Press, 1987
The Wealth of a Nation (ed, with contributions), NMS Publishing, 1989
Scotland in Trust, Richard Drew, 1990
St Ives by RL Stevenson (new ending), Richard Drew, 1990
No Ordinary Journey: John Rae, Arctic Explorer (with Ian Bunyan, Dale Idiens and Bryce Wilson), NMS Publishing, 1993
Mediterranean (poems, as Jenni Daiches), Scottish Cultural Press, 1995
The Nine Lives of Naomi Mitchison, Virago, 1997
Museum of Scotland (guidebook), NMS Publishing, 1998
Present Poets 1 (ed, poetry anthology), NMS Publishing, 1998
Translated Kingdoms (ed, poetry anthology), NMS Publishing, 1999
Robert Louis Stevenson, (poetry, ed), Everyman, 1999
Present Poets 2 (ed, poetry anthology), NMS Publishing, 2000
Not Nebuchadnezzar: In Search of Identities, Luath Press, 2005
Scots in the USA, Luath Press, 2006
Letters From the Great Wall, Luath Press, 2006
Frontier Scots: The Scots Who Won the West, Luath Press, 2010
Lost in the Backwoods: Scots and North American Wilderness, Edinburgh University Press, 2013

Scots in Canada

JENNI CALDER

Luath Press Limited

EDINBURGH

www.luath.co.uk

First published 2003
Reprinted 2008
Reprinted 2009
New edition 2013

ISBN 978-1-908373-03-8

The paper used in this book is recyclable.
It is made from low chlorine pulps produced in a low energy,
low emission manner from renewable forests.

Printed and bound by
Bell & Bain Ltd, Glasgow

Typeset in 10.5 point Sabon

Maps by Jim Lewis

Contents

Preface

The northernmost point of mainland Scotland is on approximately the same latitude as Canada's northern Labrador, Churchill on Hudson Bay and Lake Athabasca which straddles the provinces of Saskatchewan and Alberta. If you continue west you'll find yourself about 200 miles south of the Yukon, explored in the 1840s by Robert Campbell from Glen Lyon and celebrated sixty years later by Robert Service who grew up in Glasgow. Scots, particularly Highland Scots, are often described as a hardy northern people accustomed to a rugged existence and having a natural affinity with the harsh terrain and climate of much of Canada. But part of the explanation for the striking impact of Scots in Canada is more prosaic. For any ship sailing westward from Scotland on that latitude Labrador is the first landfall, although over several centuries a more likely course for Scottish ships was north into Arctic waters and Hudson Bay or south to Nova Scotia. The Hudson's Bay Company became synonymous with Scottish enterprise and resilience, while Nova Scotia was a place where thousands of Scots made their homes and is today still thick with Scottish names.

Since *Scots in Canada* was first published in 2003 there has been increasing interest in Scotland's diaspora and Scottish achievement overseas. This vast area of Scotland's past is receiving escalating academic attention, spearheaded by Professor Tom Devine at the University of Edinburgh and contributed to by many others in different parts of the world. In the last ten years there have been many new books, articles and television programmes relating to the topic.

The aim of *Scots in Canada* is to tell the story of how many thousands of Scots, impelled by a great variety of hopes, aspirations and circumstances, crossed the Atlantic and made new lives in a land which profoundly challenged their fortitude and resourcefulness. Their experiences in the vast territory that became the Dominion of Canada were also immensely varied. Some lamented their departure, others enthusiastically embraced new opportunities, and some did both. There were spectacular successes and tragic failures, but for most of those who in the eighteenth and nineteenth centuries carved out a new life in areas of unimagined wilderness it was a story of dogged survival and gradual improvement.

Whatever the particular experience of individuals and communities from Scotland, their imprint on Canada's development and institutions was indelible. Any visitor to Canada will quickly become aware of a Scottish presence. There are communities, particularly in Nova Scotia, Prince Edward Island and Ontario, which have retained a strong Scottish identity. Every year there are dozens of events that celebrate a Scottish heritage. Fergus, Ontario, for example, founded in 1833 by Adam Fergusson from Perthshire, holds an annual Highland games and festival with a packed programme of field events, pipe bands, traditional music, Highland dancing, whisky tasting, and talks, readings and demonstrations relating to Scottish history and culture. To the purist such events may at times depart from 'authenticity', but significantly they remind us of the way Scotland has been imported into Canadian life. Without the Scottish contribution Canada would be a very different place.

Many Canadians are very aware of the Scottish impact on their history. There are continual reminders on every map of Canada and in every Canadian telephone directory. Scottish names are prominent in almost every Canadian graveyard. In Scotland, we give less thought to the part Canada has played in our past. I hope that *Scots in Canada* will contribute to an understanding of the way Scotland's history reaches far beyond the country that we tend to think of as small and overshadowed by others. The Scottish experience overseas is an important strand in the way the nation defines itself, and Canada in particular offers many examples of the tenacity and resourcefulness that led to Scots often being described as ideal settlers. Many of the most significant figures in Canadian history were Scots: explorers Alexander Mackenzie, Simon Fraser and John Rae; governor of the Hudson's Bay Company George Simpson; entrepreneurs and railway builders Donald Smith (Lord Strathcona) and George Stephen (Lord Mount Stephen); first prime minister John Macdonald, and hundreds more. But there were also episodes of failure and greed, of exploitation, miscalculation and murderous rivalry. Although many Scots were respectful of the First Nations and acknowledged a frequent dependence on their skills, others were dismissive and had no qualms about displacing aboriginal peoples. The fur trade, dominated by Scots, ruthlessly exploited both the environment and the First Nations on whom it depended for the supply of pelts. Commercial imperatives, originating in Britain as well as Canada itself, drove most of the distinctive Scottish achievements in Canada.

Those commercial imperatives had an impact on Scotland as well as the New World, tempting many who saw North America as a gateway to opportunity as well as absorbing large numbers who had little choice but to leave their homeland. But the consequences for Scotland are not to be reckoned only in terms of departures and absences. The Canada connection brought prosperity to some and economic alleviation to many more. The demand for goods to supply Canadian settlement and Canadian trade was a considerable boost to the Scottish economy. Without the Hudson's Bay Company which employed hundreds of Orkneymen, Orkney communities would have struggled. The hugely important timber trade also affected life and work in Scotland. There are few Scottish families even now that are without some connection, direct or indirect, with Canada.

At a time when there is much discussion of migration, identity and nationality, it is even more important to understand how Canada fits into Scotland's story.

Jenni Calder
South Queensferry, 2013

The many ships that left our country
with white wings for Canada.
They are like handkerchiefs in our memories
and the brine like tears

CHAPTER ONE

The Ship Under Sail

*The ship is now under sail
that is to ferry me over the waves.*
JOHN SINCLAIR

FROM THE WEST coast of Harris, one of Scotland's Hebridean islands, you look out to the Atlantic Ocean. On a clear day you might see St Kilda, the most westerly piece of the British Isles. With infinite vision and the ability to bend to the curve of the earth's surface you would see the coast of Newfoundland, less than two thousand miles away. Many Scots for many hundreds of years were accustomed to the Atlantic and the notion that there was another land on its western shore. From the seventeenth century that other land became an important part of Scotland's history and Scotland contributed indelibly to the way that other land developed.

Stand by the Clyde above Port Glasgow and you can see the remnants of wooden stakes in the river. This was where rafts of Canadian timber awaited their final destination after being unloaded. The ships that made the transatlantic crossing did not sail empty to Canada but carried a lucrative cargo: people. Thousands of them departed from Greenock and small ports scattered along the west coast. They are all evidence of the Canada connection. But it is not only Scotland's west coast that looked to Canada. The east coast also saw the emigrant ships depart, particularly from Aberdeen. The east coast whaling ports, Leith, Kirkcaldy, Dundee and Peterhead, are built into the history of Arctic whaling and exploration which took Scots to the most northerly reaches of the vast territory that became Canada. Further north, Orkney's involvement with the Hudson's Bay Company is a deeply embedded facet of the islands' history. The Pier Arts Centre in Stromness, once the headquarters of the Company which recruited hundreds of Orcadians to play a part in the fur trade, and displays in the Stromness Museum are tangible reminders.

Over the centuries Scots knew of the northern expanse of the New World, or parts of it, as Nova Scotia, Upper and Lower Canada and Rupert's Land, until in 1867 the process began of combining these colonial tracts into the Dominion of Canada. Before the United States of America was born 'America' could mean anywhere from the Gulf of Mexico to the Arctic Circle. After Britain lost the Thirteen Colonies, British North America was the general designation of what became Canada. There can be few Scots families that don't have some kind of connection. At some point in the last four hundred years there is likely to have been a forebear who went to Canada or who contributed in some way to maintaining the Scottish-Canadian link. There will be someone who helped to build a ship or make a sail or unload timber or prepare a passenger list. Someone will have received a letter from Canada or woven a shawl or forged an axe that voyaged across the Atlantic.

The map of Canada is peppered with Scottish names. They have been given to rivers and mountains, towns and counties, bays and inlets. Canada's telephone directories are filled with them. Wander along the street of almost any community in Cape Breton and check the names on the mailboxes: you may find yourself thinking that it hardly seems possible that there can be Macleods or Macdonalds still in Scotland. Formative aspects of Canada's history were dominated by Scots, in particular the Hudson's Bay Company which determined so much of the character of British North America, and the Canadian Pacific Railway which made the vital coast-to-coast connection. Scottish names are prominent in the government of Canada. There are nearly five million people of Scottish descent in Canada, while Scotland's population is not a great deal more than that.

Why did so many Scots go to Canada, and having got there, what made them so prominent, in the decades of colonial settlement and in the growth of the young nation after Confederation in 1867? What was the experience of leaving Scotland and making a new life in what was for Scots a new world? To what extent did they maintain links with the old country and keep alive the cultural traditions they brought with them? The answers highlight a story of migration that has echoes all over Europe, where particularly in the nineteenth century huge numbers of people were displaced, and all over North America, where so many of them began their lives again.

Evidence of departure can be found all over Scotland. For centuries before the first significant movement of Scots to North America began Scots had been leaving to live and work elsewhere, in England of course, in Scandinavia and the Baltic states, in France, Germany and Russia. At one time it was reckoned that there were as many as 30,000 Scots settled in Poland. These European connections stamped the history of the east coast ports in particular. Leith, Culross and Crail, for example, all owed their vibrant success in the fifteenth and sixteenth centuries to the activities of Scots overseas. Scottish merchants, soldiers and scholars, and later engineers, architects and industrialists, did not hesitate to move in response to opportunities overseas. So there was a tradition of leaving Scotland long before attention was turned to the other side of the Atlantic.

It was a tradition fostered by aspiration and a sense of adventure as much as by hardship and the pressures of penury, all of which would play a part in sending Scots to Canada. Although many left because they had no choice, it is probably fair to say that most believed that they were making a journey towards a better life. Some intended that that better life should be back in Scotland, and it often happened that after a period of months or years migrating Scots returned. But not all those who intended a temporary sojourn in fact made their way back to Scotland. For a variety of reasons, the New World retained them. And some of those who did return had anticipated living out their lives in their new country, but were disillusioned or frustrated by the reality they met.

The first significant Scottish migration to Canada began in the seventeenth century with the efforts to settle Nova Scotia. Although this was a tentative start, later Nova Scotia would become a very Scottish province. Emigration to America generally gathered pace in the eighteenth century, particularly in the second half, spurred by the enforced exile of defeated Jacobites and by the need for British soldiers to fight colonial wars in North America. After the defeat of Charles Edward Stewart's Jacobite army at Culloden in 1746 the displacement of Highlanders overseas became official policy, as punishment in the first instance, and then as recruitment. The Jacobites went mainly to the Thirteen Colonies, where there were already numbers of Scots, including communities of Gaelic-speaking Highlanders. Among them were Jacobites who had been transported to South Carolina after the Rising of 1715 as well as groups of Highlanders who had left voluntarily. However, the potential of Highlanders as a fighting force was acknowledged, as was the usefulness of recruiting disaffected young men into the army and removing them from their native territory, where they might cause trouble. Highland regiments were raised and sent to fight overseas. The French were the enemy from 1756, and with the end in 1763 of the French and Indian Wars (the American end of the Seven Years War), North America was secured for Britain. Many Scottish soldiers took advantage of the offer of land grants along the St Lawrence River.

The abundant fishing grounds off Newfoundland had early attracted the attention of Europeans, including Scots, who joined those crossing the Atlantic to fish. Some efforts were made to encourage Scots to settle there. An advertisement of 1771 in the *Glasgow Journal* painted an enticing picture:

> Any person inclining to make their fortune and live happily in the island of St John's Newfoundland where the soil is excellent and a good healthy climate, great plenty of stone and timber and lime within a few leagues of water carriage, the sea and rivers full of fish.

But although some Scots did settle in Newfoundland, notably in the mid-nineteenth century when a number moved on from Nova Scotia, it never became a prime destination for emigrant Scots.

When in 1775 the Thirteen Colonies signalled rebellion against George III and British rule, the majority of Highland settlers in the Colonies, along with those Scots who had a vested interest in the status quo, supported the king. With British defeat, the Loyalists became refugees and most made their way to Nova Scotia, New Brunswick and Quebec. There were about 40,000 of them. Some joined existing communities, others went to new areas of settlement. They received considerable government support, in the form of land grants in good locations, clothing, household goods and tools. The Loyalists were a special case; many had not chosen to leave Scotland in the first place, and none had chosen Canada as their destination. Those from the southern colonies found the north very different in climate and terrain, and the work involved in starting all over again could be discouragingly hard.

But many of Canada's eighteenth-century settlers left Scotland willingly to go to their chosen destination. The factors that influenced their choice were mixed. Dissatisfaction with circumstances at home and hope for a better life combined in varying proportions. Fluctuating economic conditions played a part. In the 1770s, for example, a crisis in the Lowland textile industry, which had been employing increasing numbers, encouraged textile workers to look to North America for new opportunities. In the same decade poor harvests and rising rents meant that those dependent on the land, especially in the Highlands, were struggling. Emigration was tempting. It was also expensive, particularly for those who played no part in the cash economy. Most Highland tenants had little opportunity to handle money, and if they wanted to leave were reliant on what they could raise by selling their stock and any possessions they could not take with them. Nevertheless, many of those who departed Scotland were able both to pay their fares and to take with them sufficient cash and goods to get them started. One of the main arguments against emigration was that it not only took the most energetic and enterprising individuals out of Scotland, it also removed capital. Scotland was being drained of human and financial resources.

The totally destitute, who were seen as an encumbrance rather than a resource, were not in a position to leave and anyway rarely had the will to start a new life. It was a decision not readily taken by those who had resigned themselves to a life of deprivation, who no longer had much hope that circumstances could change. Although illusions persisted of the New World promising an easy life, there was an increasing flow of information coming back to Scotland about conditions and requirements. Those who had gone before wrote letters, and literature offering advice began to be published. Travellers returned with accounts of their experiences, and Scots generally expressed considerable interest in the other side of the Atlantic. An increasing number had good reason to, as commercial as well as personal connections grew.

What fuelled the hope for a better life? A key factor was the prospect of owning land. The pace of agricultural modernisation was accelerating in the eighteenth century, driven by commercial pressures and a zeal for improvement. The impact on farm labourers and tenant farmers was profound. In both Highlands and Lowlands farms were being enlarged and rationalised. With the fragmentation of the clan system, which had begun before the Jacobite Rising of 1745 but became irreversible thereafter, the old Highland small-scale subsistence farming no longer had a framework and support system. Traditional tenure of the land was eroded. The possibility of owning land on which to raise crops and stock, of never again paying rent or being subject to the demands of a landlord was an enticing prospect. As *Chambers Edinburgh Journal* put it in March 1834, Canada offered the prospect of 'the poorest becoming a possessor of the soil, earning competence for himself, and comfortably settling his children'. Only emigration could make this real. Only in a territory with unclaimed acres could a family of modest means hope to take the future into their own hands.

There were other enticements. Settler society was seen as more open, less bound by class and status, more welcoming to those with enterprise and determination. For those who were not tempted by the republican United States (and many were) British North America offered an attractive alternative. It had all the vigour and potential of a pioneer country, but was still British. For Highland communities overtaken by the new commercialism, which threatened traditional culture as well as traditional work patterns, it offered the opportunity of sustaining the old ways. A substantial amount of Highland emigration involved the transplanting of whole communities, with their kinship connections and collective memory intact. Throughout Scotland it was common for emigrants to leave and settle as families, often extended families of several generations, and for new settlers to encourage other family members to join them.

Practical factors were also important. As emigration increased in the nineteenth century the level of support, from government, from landowners desperate to rid themselves of what they saw as the burden of unproductive tenants, from the colonial government, from agents and land speculators, could make all the difference to the potential emigrant. Often the support was somewhat illusory, or so short-term as to be of limited use, but generally by the time that was discovered it was too late to turn back. Many people had vested interests in encouraging emigration: landowners on both sides of the Atlantic, ship owners, agents who pocketed a commission with every passage sold, settler communities in need of particular skills. Some were unscrupulous, but all tried very hard to ensure that British North America received a good press.

In the early 1770s there was public concern at what the *Glasgow Journal* called the 'ruinous practice' of emigration. There were calls for action to prevent it, and worries that the large numbers leaving would lead to the colonies separating themselves from Britain. There was not, however, a unified or consistent policy on emigration. Although the first organised clearances of tenants from Highland and Island estates were under way before the end of the eighteenth century, the realisation of the economic value of kelp meant that many Highland lairds were doing their best to hang on to their labour force. Kelp is a seaweed found in abundance on Scotland's west coast. Its ash is a source of alkali that was important in bleaching linen and in soap and glass making. When the import of Spanish barilla, also derived from seaweed, was first subjected to duty and then interrupted by the Napoleonic Wars, the price of Scottish kelp shot up. Gathering and burning the kelp was labour intensive, and Hebridean landowners seeking to maximise their profits were anxious to deter their people from leaving. But the kelp bonanza – about 7,000 tons were produced in 1810 – was short-lived, and when the duty was dropped in 1825 the price plummeted and the kelp workers became redundant.

MacNeil of Barra did well out of kelp. The profits allowed him to build a fine new house and maintain a sophisticated lifestyle. The minister of Barra was able to report in the *Old Statistical Account* of 1794 that 'the spirit for emigration is now happily and totally suppressed'. But that was optimistic, as in 1817, with Napoleon defeated and worsening economic conditions, emigration was on the agenda again. Colonel MacNeil commented, 'the loss of so many very decent people, is much to be regretted: at the same time, those that remain, will in time, be much better.' Colonel MacNeil seems to have had a genuine concern for his tenants. His son, who inherited the estate at his father's death, had a very different attitude. He demanded that his tenants did what they were told – 'I must have fishers and helpers who will cheerfully do my bidding,' he wrote in 1825 to Father Angus MacDonald, the priest on Barra – and stated his intention of kicking out those who didn't. John MacCodrum, who went to Cape Breton, made his views clear in poetry written in his native Gaelic: 'Since they won't put up with you living within your familiar bounds, it's better for you to leave of your own accord, than to be oppressed like serfs.'

The landowners' interests were represented by the Highland Society based in London which lobbied effectively on their behalf. The result was the Passenger Act of 1803. On the face of it, this was an effort to improve shipboard conditions. It restricted the number of passengers a ship could carry and included regulations on provisioning and medical care. The result, inevitably, was a steep rise in the cost of passage to North America, which deterred people from leaving. The price of a ticket from the West Highlands to Nova Scotia rose from £4 to £10. Subsequent Passenger Acts reflected the policy on emigration at the time.

Emigration to North America faltered during the American revolutionary war (which confirmed the worst fears of those who warned of the link between emigration and a spirit of independence) and again in 1812 when the youthful United States invaded Canada. Britain successfully repelled the invading Americans and secured a British future for its surviving colonies, although there was more argument to come about the delineation of the border. Disbanded soldiers were again rewarded with land grants. With the collapse of the kelp industry and the intensification of clearance of large tracts of the Highlands to make way for sheep runs, the numbers of displaced and dispossessed increased dramatically. Landowners who in the early years of the nineteenth century were anxious to retain a working population were now encouraging and often forcing departure. Families already struggling to make a living from pitifully unproductive land faced increased rents and diminishing support from clan leaders who had traditionally been the guardians of their people. Many tenants submitted reluctantly to these pressures by choosing to emigrate. Many others had no choice. They were evicted from their homes, in some but not all cases with their passage paid to the other side of the Atlantic, but often with little regard for what happened to them when they got there.

The emigration of Highland communities had begun in the first half of the eighteenth century, largely as a response to rising rents and organised by clan tacksmen, the tenants of larger areas of land who sublet to others. The economic depression of the 1770s spurred departures, commented on by James Boswell and Samuel Johnson when they made their famous 1773 tour to the Highlands and Islands, and by Thomas Pennant who was there in 1769. Johnson noted that 'whole neighbourhoods formed parties for removal; so that departure from their native country is no longer exile... they change nothing but the place of their abode; and of that change they perceive the benefit'. Pennant is much less sanguine. He had sharp words for Highland landlords whom he characterised as both rapacious and neglectful. In his *Tour of Scotland and a Voyage to the Hebrides* (1769) he cautioned them to support their tenants, and not to 'force them into a distant land, and necessitate them to seek tranquillity by a measure which was once deemed the punishment of the most atrocious criminals'.

It already seemed that emigration was spreading like an epidemic but it was another few decades before wholesale clearances emptied Highland straths and glens, destroyed communities and sent hundreds of families at a time to Canada. One of the most notorious of these systematic evictions was instigated by the Countess of Sutherland in the early 1800s. In 1846 another swathe of devastation struck with the failure of the potato crop. In spite of efforts to provide organised relief for those who were literally starving the belief of many was that the land simply could not sustain its population and that the only solution was that it should leave. 'I see no prospect of relief for the population, without emigration,' said Charles McQuarrie, a merchant in Mull. The cost of passage overseas was raised by landlords and public subscription, though even in these extreme circumstances there was often profound resistance to leaving.

Further south, Scotland's growing industrial areas were also producing economic casualties. The mechanisation of industry was perhaps even more relentless than the commercialising of agriculture, and was just as callous towards the labour force. In the early decades of the nineteenth century a key contributor to Scotland's economic success was the textile industry, but mechanised weaving, for all the large numbers employed in the factories, was putting hundreds of handloom weavers out of work. It was among the weavers that some of the first emigration societies were formed in the 1820s. In that decade around eighty societies came into being, which were responsible for getting around two thousand people to Canada. The societies were set up mainly by weavers in or near Glasgow. All saw the benefits of acting collectively and providing mutual support. The government was petitioned for assistance, and charitable organisations also helped. In 1820 the government responded by providing a loan of £11,000 to enable 1,100 individuals to go to Upper Canada. Included in the deal was free transport for their onward journey from Quebec, a 100-acre land grant for each family, with seed corn and tools provided.

As more Scots made the journey west, more information flowed back. Throughout the century, the tone of letters to family and friends at home ranged from the demoralised to the highly satisfied. They often included useful practical information about what to bring and what to leave behind. Increasing numbers of pamphlets and books were published, offering a picture of what emigrants could expect and freighted with advice. William Bell's *Hints to Emigrants* (1824) warns against the 'flattering accounts' of Canada people may have seen, but nevertheless encourages emigration. 'Your surplus population, who have not employment at home, could not do better than come to Canada, provided they are possessed of health, industry, perseverance, and as much cash as to settle them decently upon their land'. He made it clear that emigration is not for the faint-hearted or for the impecunious. John Galt, instrumental in founding the town of Guelph in Upper Canada in 1827, delivered his emigrant's guide in the form of a novel, *Bogle Corbet, or The Emigrants* (1831). He makes his intentions clear: 'it contains instruction that may help to lighten the anxieties of those whom taste or fortune prompts to quit their native land, and to seek in the wilderness new objects of industry, enterprise, and care'.

Reports on British North America often stressed the rigours of the climate. Robert MacDougall published his Gaelic *Emigrant's Guide to North America* in 1841, and was literally at a lost for words to describe his experience of the cold:

> ... any man who has never been away from Scotland may talk, read, imagine, and dream of cold until he goes grey, but as long as he lives, he will not comprehend the extent of the cold in Canada until he himself feels it or another cold equal to it. My ears have felt it, but though they have, I have no words to describe its harshness, as in truth, the Gaelic language is not capable of describing it.

Alexander Buchanan, the government chief immigration agent whose task it was to assist intending settlers when they arrived, produced detailed practical advice on maintaining good health while adjusting to the new environment:

> Dress yourself in light clean clothing... Cut your hair short, and wash daily and thoroughly. Avoid drinking ardent spirits of any kind, and when heated do not drink cold water. Eat moderately of light food. Avoid night dews.

Catherine Parr Traill in her *Female Emigrant's Guide and Hints on Canadian Housekeeping* (1854) takes up the theme of perseverance and hard work, which she reiterates throughout. 'In Canada persevering energy and industry, with sobriety, will overcome all obstacles, and in time will place the very poorest family in a position of substantial comfort that no personal exertions alone could have procured for them elsewhere.' Her message was that even the destitute could succeed if they tried hard enough.

One of the most remarkable migration stories is that of the group who were led by the Reverend Norman McLeod, a breakaway Presbyterian who had a following in Sutherland and Wester Ross. Prevented from preaching and taking up a post as parish schoolmaster in Ullapool, in 1817 he and 400 followers built their own boat and set off across the Atlantic. They arrived at Pictou, but McLeod soon had the Presbyterian church there in a state of agitation – he was an immensely popular preacher and severely critical of any apparent laxness – and after three years he and his followers were building another boat. The plan was to go to Ohio but off Cape Breton Island storms intervened. McLeod and the 200 who had stuck with him changed their plans and established a settlement in St Ann's Bay in the northeast of the island. McLeod was an exacting and authoritarian leader, who not only held his people together but fired them to migrate yet again, this time to Australia and eventually to New Zealand, where they founded a community at Waipu on North Island.

Not everyone who left Scotland went to Canada, of course, but it remained throughout the century the favoured destination. The United States was also attractive, especially to the independently-minded, and by the mid-century Australia was becoming an increasingly popular destination. But crossing the Atlantic was not so daunting a prospect as voyaging half way round the world, and Scots generally knew a great deal more about Canada than about Australia or New Zealand. In 1849 *The Scotsman* reckoned that 20,000 Highlanders had emigrated to Canada in the previous decade, and the more who went the more attractive the proposition became. If kith and kin were already established it was easier to make the decision to uproot and join them, or to accept the inevitable when emigration was enforced.

The growing perception of the Highlands and Islands as over-populated became even stronger with the potato famine of the 1840s. In spite of the efforts made on the part of the government and the church to provide relief, in many areas it seemed that the only solution was to decrease the numbers on the land. There was another wave of organised emigration. Landlords evicted those seen as surplus to requirements or who hindered their vision of prosperity. Some paid passage to Canada, but that was only a small part of what was required to enable settlement. The Duke of Argyll made it clear that it was worth his while to finance the departure of those whom he would otherwise feel obliged to support. Among the most notorious evictions were those instituted by John Gordon of Cluny, who got rid of tenants in Barra (where he had bought the MacNeil estate), South Uist and Benbecula. In 1851 he sent over sixteen hundred to Quebec, but made no provision for them to get to Upper Canada. They had no resources themselves with which to continue their journey or begin their new lives, and many of them spoke only Gaelic. Alexander Buchanan, the government chief immigration agent, had to pick up the pieces and vigorously condemned the irresponsibility of landlords who so cynically sent their people into the unknown. As it was impossible to allow thousands of destitute and bewildered Gaels to remain in Quebec, the government had no choice but to provide the means of sending them on to their ultimate destination and supporting their settlement.

The 1850s saw a new threat to crofting survival, the turning of vast areas of the Highlands into sporting estates. This brought more clearances; by 1884 there were nearly two million acres of deer forest. 'Why should we emigrate?' asked Donald Macdonald of Back of Keppoch. 'There is plenty of waste land around us; for what is an extensive deer-forest in the heart of the most fertile part of our land but waste land?' The grievances of Highland and Island crofters intensified and the early 1880s erupted into rent strikes and land raids. Protest was focused through the Highland Land League, formed in 1883. The Crofting Act of 1886 brought a measure of reform, securing fairer rents and security of tenure, but crofters remained without sufficient land to subsist, and the act did nothing to help landless labourers. The tide of emigration continued.

It continued also in the Lowlands, where changing land use and increasingly industrialised agriculture displaced tenants and labourers. Many left Scotland altogether, choosing a life that offered some hope of advancement over an existence of low wages and poor conditions. 'These men,' commented the *Aberdeen Herald* in 1852, 'in many cases, have been obliged, along with their families, to take refuge in our towns, or have emigrated to countries where their skill and industry will be more highly appreciated.' Some went to Canada to work temporarily, on the canals and railroads, as masons and builders, and then returned to Scotland. The advent of steam, which meant that the transatlantic passage was both faster and less dependent on weather conditions, made this feasible. Crossing the Atlantic was no longer as final as it once had seemed. Steam also created jobs and opportunities in Canada.

JM Bumsted has estimated that in the thirty years from 1871, 80,000 Scots went to Canada. These were the decades after Confederation, when the newly created Dominion of Canada was energetically encouraging settlement, especially in the prairie provinces. Agents were active in Scotland, tempting emigrants with an enticing vision of land and prosperity. The agents were mainly Canadian Scots, and several were Gaelic speakers. They travelled extensively, giving illustrated lectures, distributing literature and making themselves available to answer questions. Angus Nicholson, for example, was based in the Highlands between 1872 and 1875. He lectured in Glasgow, Greenock, Rothesay and Perth as well as visiting Skye, Lewis, Harris and Uist. He claimed credit for deflecting intending emigrants from destinations in the USA and New Zealand to Canada. A hundred years after clearances were beginning to depopulate the West Highlands, Nicholson identified this area as still being 'over-peopled', as so much land had been given over to 'sheep, deer and English pleasure grounds'.

Although the stream of pamphlets, guides and general accounts of Canada diminished in the second half of the century, their percentage of emigration literature as a whole increased. The focus was no longer Nova Scotia and the newly-named provinces of Quebec and Ontario, but Manitoba, and more of the publications were coming from Canada itself. *Manitoba, and the Northwest of the Dominion: Its Resources and Advantages to the Emigrant and Capitalist, as Compared with the Western States of America*, by Thomas Spence (Quebec, 1876), shows how vigorously Manitoba was aiming to attract people of substance and to compete with the attractions of the United States. The following year Alexander Begg published a *Practical Hand-book and Guide to Manitoba and the Northwest* in Toronto. In 1879 Thomas Spence produced a second title, reiterating the message: *The Prairie Lands of Canada: Presented to the World as a New and Inviting Field of Enterprise for the Capitalist, and New Superior Attractions and Advantages as a Home for Immigrants Compared with the Western Prairies of the United States.* This was at a time when throughout Europe increasing numbers of the displaced and destitute were looking to the New World as a place of refuge.

From the Emigrants' Information Office and the Emigration Commission in London came regular publications which provided information on colonial destinations and how to get there. A poster of 1889 gives information on passage to Canada, along with Australia, New Zealand and South Africa, landing arrangements and the demand for labour. Canada is identified as needing 'farmers with capital', 'farm labourers' and 'female domestic servants'. For the potential emigrant Canada was clearly still a very attractive prospect. Passage by steamer took nine to ten days, compared with twice as long to the Cape and five times as long, or three months by sail, to New South Wales. Although at this time there was no government assisted passage, the cost of crossing the Atlantic was a great deal less than the cost of getting to any other colonial destination. A pamphlet printed in Gaelic included 'before' and 'after' pictures to illustrate the transformation from frontier to ordered settlement that emigrants could expect. Manitoba attracted not only new emigrants, but those of an earlier generation who had settled in Nova Scotia or Ontario.

Unlike the United States and Australia, British North America was not used as a dumping ground for criminals and rebels (although undesirables of other kinds were certainly dumped there), and it was only rarely an arena for the indentured servant system, which involved individuals being tied for a specified period of time to work for a particular master. But it did become a destination for those who were seen as actual or potential burdens to society. Canada was identified as a suitable destination for orphans and destitute children, and from the 1870s there were several schemes which sent Scottish youngsters to families in Canada. Some were well looked after and flourished. Others were exploited as unpaid labour. Conditions could be very poor and siblings were often split up. For older children there were training schemes which prepared them for work, mainly on the land or in domestic service.

Between 1901 and 1914, 240,000 Scots went to Canada, and substantial numbers continued to leave after the end of World War 1, some 200,000 between 1919 and 1930. The Empire Settlement Act of 1922 provided for assisted passage for those wishing to emigrate, and there were several large-scale departures, for example those who sailed on the *Metagama* and the *Marloch* from Stornoway and Lochboisdale in 1923 and '24. They responded to a campaign sponsored by both the British and Canadian governments organised at a time when there was widespread unemployment and demoralisation in the Western Isles. Many were war veterans or members of families that had lost a son or father in the war. The call was for farm labourers and domestic servants, destined for Alberta, still actively developing new settlements, and Ontario, where old settlements were being depleted by the movement west.

Steam power, the telegraph and the telephone made it easier to communicate between Scotland and Canada, but it remained a severe wrench to depart from friends and family and the environment in which most had probably lived and worked all their lives. The earliest emigrants understood that they would never see the old country again (although some, in fact, returned) and unless they were literate, and many were not, staying in touch with those they left behind was difficult. But before they began the process of settlement, they had in front of them a daunting voyage. Although Scotland was a maritime nation, many would never have been to sea, indeed would never have been more than a few miles from the place of their birth. Some of those who sailed on the *Metagama* in 1923 had never been off the island of Lewis.

Conditions on the early emigrant ships were often appalling, over-crowded, poorly provisioned and breeding grounds of disease. The quarters on some ships were described as being worse than those of the slave-traders. On the timber ships accommodation was hastily and sketchily converted to carry passengers rather than freight; the quarters were cramped, dirty and airless. Some ship masters stinted rations in order to make a profit from the surplus. The voyage across the Atlantic might take five or six weeks or even longer, and it was common for there to be deaths – and sometimes births – at sea. Children were particularly vulnerable.

The *Bachelor*, chartered in 1773 from James Inglis, Leith, allowed 4 lbs of meal, 5 lbs of bread biscuit, 2 lbs of beef, 2 lbs of barley and pease, 1 lb molasses and 6 gallons of water per adult passenger per week. Children under eight had half rations. Passage cost £6 for adults and £3 for children. The *Fortune* left Skye in 1791 with 480 people on board. Their accommodation consisted of bunks 18 inches wide and 2 feet of head room: this was standard. There were two pots for cooking the inadequate provision of food. The *Sarah* and the *Dove* left Fort William for Nova Scotia in 1801, carrying 700 passengers. The voyage took thirteen weeks and provisions were meagre. Smallpox and whooping cough killed nearly fifty. The Robertson family left Aberdeen for Lower Canada in April 1846. In the midst of bad weather Mrs Robertson, who had been suffering from dysentery, gave birth to a daughter. The next day the child died and was buried at sea with 'two stones attached to it to make it sink', as her thirteen-year-old brother Charles recorded in a letter, and a few days later her mother followed her.

In April 1817 the Reverend William Bell sailed from Leith on the *Rothiemurchus*, in order to take up a post as minister at Perth, Upper Canada. In his *Hints to Emigrants* he describes his voyage. He and his wife and six children had superior accommodation in the stern, separate from the steerage passengers, although the partition promised by the captain was never constructed. Most of the passengers had neither space nor privacy:

On each side of the ship were ranged two tiers or stories of bed-births; the passengers providing their own bedding. Along the open space in the middle were placed two rows of large chests, which were sometimes used as tables, and at other times as seats.

There was confusion as people scrambled for the best berths, and the captain, as Bell put it, 'was obliged to interpose his authority'. 'The crying of the children, the swearing of the sailors, and the scolding of the women who had not got the beds they wanted, produced a concert in which it was difficult to discover any harmony.'

There was a daily serving of soup, but the captain was found to be withholding flour, oatmeal and butter to which the passengers were entitled. Eventually he consented with bad grace to providing these. By the time they were in sight of Cape Breton the beef, loaded at Leith, had deteriorated, and the soup was described as 'merely stinking water, in which stinking beef had been boiled, which no dog would taste unless he was starving'. Departure from an east coast port had added two weeks and the stormy Pentland Firth to the voyage. It was a relief to glimpse the western shore, although not entirely encouraging. Icebergs loomed as they approached Newfoundland. Cape Breton appeared to be 'mountainous, rocky and barren, and was partially covered with snow' – this was in May. There was ice in the Gulf of St Lawrence.

Like most emigrants to Upper Canada, the Bells' initial destination was Quebec, which they reached in early June, but they still had a considerable journey ahead of them. Many emigrants arrived with no knowledge of how to reach their intended destination, and little money to pay their way. Travel was mainly by water, and for most Montreal was the next stage. The Bells continued their journey up the St Lawrence in some comfort, on the *Malsham*, which offered accommodation much superior to that on the *Rothiemurchus*. The quarters were spacious, with a separate cabin for the ladies, and provisions were 'abundant in quantity... and excellent in quality'. It took thirty-six hours to travel the 180 miles upriver. They continued their journey by cart to Lachine, in order to avoid the notorious rapids that lay beyond Montreal, then onwards by open boat, with numerous portages, to Prescott. These Durham boats were clumsy and slow and had to be dragged through the rapids, the passengers decanted to walk alongside. 'I had no idea,' wrote Bell, 'that the ascent of the St Lawrence was attended with so much labour and difficulty.' Bell's family and their luggage made the last stage of the journey, from Prescott to Perth, by wagon, with Bell himself riding on ahead. Leith to Perth, Upper Canada, took them over two months. Many emigrants made a much longer journey, in both time and miles, and a much less comfortable one.

Concerns about disease, especially cholera, prompted the setting up in 1831 of a quarantine station at Grosse Ile on the St Lawrence, thirty miles downriver from Quebec. Every emigrant ship had to be checked, unless it had already been certified as free from disease. Passengers showing symptoms were disembarked and admitted to the hospital. The combination of insanitary shipboard conditions and malnourishment among the passengers increased the likelihood of disease crossing the Atlantic.

Large numbers of ships bound for North America left from the west coast, with Greenock the key departure point although ships picked up passengers at Highland and Island ports from Stornoway to Campbeltown. But east coast ports also saw American departures, particularly Aberdeen, with Leith, too, having a longstanding connection with the North American trade. Ports in the north of Scotland, such as Thurso and Cromarty, also saw transatlantic departures. In June 1831 there were three ships lying off Cromarty to pick up passengers, about 700 in all. The price of a ticket across the Atlantic was two guineas, and passengers had to provide their own food. That year six emigrant ships sailed from Cromarty.

Not all Scottish emigrants left from Scotland. It was common to travel from the Clyde to Liverpool and join a transatlantic vessel there. Some people departed from the south of England. Many emigrant ships were lost at sea, some certainly because they were not seaworthy, although efforts were made through successive Passenger Acts to ensure some kind of regulation. From 1847 to 1853 at least forty-nine emigrant ships went down. By the 1850s ocean-going steamships were replacing sail. Steam made a huge difference to the experience of crossing the Atlantic. Conditions could still be fetid and overcrowded and the food terrible but at least the voyage was likely to be over in nine or ten days. Steam brought a decline in transatlantic shipping out of Aberdeen and smaller ports, while the volume of shipping out of Greenock expanded. By the 1850s the Allan Line, founded by Alexander Allan of Saltcoats and operating from the Clyde, was the major passenger service between Scotland and Quebec.

Over 300 years thousands of Scots disembarked at Pictou and Charlottetown, Halifax and Saint John, Quebec and Montreal. Many arrived demoralised, malnourished and anxious. Many had been wrenched protesting from their homes, or had been bullied, cheated and exploited. Some had lost a loved one on the voyage. But there were also those who would have agreed with John Galt's Bogle Corbet: 'Impatient with the circumstances of the old world, how wretched would the present generation have been, had not an asylum opened up for so many of us across the Atlantic.' Even those looking forward with hopeful anticipation to their new lives could hardly have been without apprehension. Although some would fail, the vast majority made a decent living although they often endured several years of discouragement and backbreaking work; more than a few were strikingly successful. Their experiences and their personalities made an indelible imprint on Canada's history.

CHAPTER TWO

Land and Habitation

We will get land and habitation
in the wilderness yonder.
RED RORY MACKENZIE

FIVE HUNDRED MILLION years ago Nova Scotia and Scotland were
part of the same landmass. In his story 'The Road to Rankin's
Point' Alistair MacLeod describes a rocky headland with the
sea crashing against the foot of the cliffs. At the roadside there
are alder and silver birch, thistles and wild roses, bluebells and
wild raspberries. There are vestiges of stone walls and the granite
foundations of houses. There are sheep and collie dogs. To those
familiar with the Scottish Highlands it could be a place they think
they know, a place where there was once perhaps a community but
is now occupied by a single croft or farm. But this isn't Scotland,
it is Cape Breton.

James VI of Scotland and I of England had ideas about colonies
and settlement, which in 1608 he put into effect with the settlement
of Scots in Ulster. The colony he encouraged at Jamestown in
Virginia was an English enterprise, although in the longer term it
served Scots extremely well as they were to become leading players
in the tobacco trade. But Scots also had a role in early transatlantic
settlement, which began in Nova Scotia. In 1621 James granted
Sir William Alexander of Menstrie a charter for a large chunk
of North America that included present-day Nova Scotia and
New Brunswick. Sir William had grand ideas of a 'new Scotland'
furnishing riches to be sent back to the mother country, just as the

New World was proving a treasure house for England and Spain. Not much attention was given to the fact that these territories were already inhabited, principally by the Mi'kmaq, Malecite and Passamaquoddy people.

Alexander's initial attempts at settlement failed. He allotted Cape Breton and Prince Edward Island to Sir Robert Gordon of Lochinvar, who named the area New Galloway and organised the first Scottish expedition to Nova Scotia, which proved abortive. In spite of, or perhaps because of, this lack of success, both William Alexander and Robert Gordon wrote pamphlets aimed at encouraging settlement in Nova Scotia. 'Where was ever Ambition baited with greater hopes than here, or where ever had Virtue so large a field to reape the fruits of Glory,' wrote Sir William in his *Encouragement to Colonists*. He saw colonies as providing an occupation for younger sons as well as bringing economic benefit to Scotland. In the event, he lost his own investment in the scheme and it would be another few years before Nova Scotia became, for Scotland, more than a name.

The Scots were not the first Europeans in Nova Scotia. The French were there before them. In 1603 Samuel de Champlain had sailed up the St Lawrence River (piloted by Abraham Martin, a Scot) as far as what would become Montreal, and the following year Port Royal (now Annapolis Royal) on the Bay of Fundy was established as a French settlement. The French gave the name 'Acadie', or Acadia, to the territory. In 1608 they founded Quebec. Over a hundred colonists settled at Port Royal, but at Quebec after twelve years there were still only sixty people, and the French foothold in Canada remained precarious. In 1613 they lost Port Royal to the British.

James vi came up with another plan to promote a hold on Canada, the selling of Nova Scotia baronetcies. The baronetcies entitled the holder to land in Nova Scotia (resigned to the Crown by Sir William Alexander), on condition that the land was settled. The scheme did not in fact get under way until James's son Charles 1 was on the throne. The baronets paid 3000 marks for their title which brought them around 10,000 acres. It was up to them to get together the finance, the people and the equipment actually to settle the land. The scheme was not a great success as most of the baronets – 113 had been created by 1638 – went nowhere near Nova Scotia, but in 1629 William Alexander's son, also William, set off on another attempt to plant Scots in Nova Scotia. With him was James Stewart of Ochiltree who with fifty people landed on Cape Breton Island. Alexander himself went to Port Royal. Three years later Port Royal was returned to France and the colonists had to move.

In 1713 the Treaty of Utrecht gave Nova Scotia to Britain, but that wasn't the end of the French in Canada. For the next fifty years 'New Scotland' was a great deal more French than Scottish. The French retained Cape Breton Island, and built a strategically-positioned fort at Louisbourg in the southeast corner. In 1755 the French were expelled from Acadia, and the Treaty of Paris which marked the end of the Seven Years War confirmed the North American colonies as British, although French-speaking settlements remained. When Britain lost the Thirteen Colonies, British North America became the term used to distinguish the territory that lay to the north of the original United States.

England and France had long been competing for the abundant Newfoundland fishing grounds, with fishing boats crossing the Atlantic on a seasonal basis and establishing footholds on the coast. Only between May and September were Newfoundland waters free of ice. By the early eighteenth century Scots were participating in a lucrative trade, with ships out of Greenock taking on cargoes of dried cod in Newfoundland and heading south for the Caribbean. Although there was awareness of the economic potential of Newfoundland, it didn't attract settlement in the same way as Nova Scotia, where the Scottish presence was gradually strengthening. The legacy of war gave it a powerful boost. Part of the boost was the displacement of the Acadians, which vacated land. Americans were invited to take it up, and among those who responded were about 600 Ulster Scots (the descendants of Scots who settled in Northern Ireland in the seventeenth century) from New Hampshire, who were later joined by more from Ulster.

Several Scottish regiments fought in the Seven Years War (not only in America, but in Europe and India) and in the American War of Independence. At the end of the former, many disbanded soldiers elected to stay in the colonies, including Nova Scotia, enticed by land grants and government support, and knowing that there was not much for them at home. This was not just a matter of rewards for soldiering; there were strategic advantages in settlement. Men of Fraser's Highlanders settled along the St Lawrence and also in Prince Edward Island, known then as the island of St John. In Prince Edward Island sixty-seven townships of 20,000 acres each had been designated. The usual system was that in return for a substantial land grant proprietors undertook to bring in colonists within a stipulated period of time. As well as being necessary to develop the land it was the only way most proprietors could pay for it. Often, however, the land was neither settled nor paid for. It was a huge and expensive undertaking to bring people out from Scotland, and it required propaganda as well as organisation. Disbanded soldiers provided a particularly useful vanguard, as they had some knowledge of the territory and attracted family and friends to join them.

Sir James Montgomery acquired a large holding of land in Prince Edward Island and set about arranging settlement. In April 1770 a group of sixty, mainly from Perthshire, left Greenock on the *Falmouth*. They leased land for one shilling an acre, which seemed an attractive proposition. But they had to supply their own provisions and materials and it took them two years to clear the densely forested land and build houses. Montgomery was fully aware of the exploitation involved: he referred to the settlers as 'white negroes'. Not surprisingly, many abandoned the island for the mainland. Also in 1770 the *Annabella* left Kintyre with sixty families destined for the Island, and the following year the *Edinburgh* with a hundred emigrants. In July 1771 Captain Dugald Stewart of Campbeltown was writing, in a letter printed in the *Glasgow Journal*, 'what a fine farm I have and what a neat house I have built, with barns and every other conveniency'. He added that he expected more settlers to come over 'as we are told they are oppressed by their lairds; and here they will be lairds themselves'.

Captain John Macdonald of Glenaladale, a Clanranald chieftain, was another who acquired a Prince Edward Island township and in 1772 took out 300 emigrants, many from Uist who were escaping pressure from their landlord to give up their Catholicism. Captain Macdonald provided free passage and, in sharp contrast to Sir James Montgomery, supplied clothing and tools and a year's provisions. He underestimated neither the difficulty of getting established nor the resources of the people he was assisting. His investment was very considerable, the cost of a 20,000-acre estate and of supporting a large number of people who had very little. He seems to have taken seriously his responsibilities as chieftain of a transplanted clan, and attempted to sustain a traditional Highland system in difficult circumstances. In 1775 he recruited men to join the Royal Highland Emigrants, a regiment raised to fight for the British in the War of Independence.

By 1780, only sixteen of the sixty-seven Island townships had been settled. Attracting people, and the whole difficult and often dangerous business of getting them across the Atlantic, were problems. In 1775 Robert Stewart of Campbeltown had arranged for Argyll emigrants to take passage on the *Elizabeth,* an old and unseaworthy ship which was wrecked off the Prince Edward Island shore. Although the passengers survived it was not a promising start to a new life, and hardly encouraged others to follow. The next milepost on the route to Prince Edward Island settlement came in 1803 when Thomas Douglas, Earl of Selkirk, began to put into practice his ambitious ideas for colonisation which he saw as an essential strategy for the relief of struggling Highlanders. It was an issue which dominated the rest of his life and which involved, at least initially, acting in the face of landlord opposition to emigration. The lack of take-up of Island land grants enabled him to secure lots cheaply which he divided into 50- to 100-acre sections and proposed to sell for two to four shillings an acre.

Selkirk's initial intention had been to found a settlement in Upper Canada, but the government withdrew the offer of land. In the meantime he had recruited 800 emigrants from Skye, the Uists and Mull. He advanced money for their passage and the tools and seed they needed to get started, and accompanied them across the Atlantic. Although the first reaction of one them as Prince Edward Island came into view was distinctly negative – 'the appearance of the country, viewed from the deck of the ship, was so wild and uncultivated, that it struck a damp upon us all' – when Selkirk returned the following year he was impressed. 'I found the settlers engaged in securing the harvest which their industry had procured,' he wrote. The land was being cleared and cultivated, and boats had been built for fishing. According to Selkirk, the settlement was already self-sufficient. 'To their industrious dispositions and persevering energy, the highest praise is due', he commented.

Selkirk did manage to get the Upper Canada settlement under way, although it faltered very quickly, but he is best known for the colony he established at Red River several years later. This was his most ambitious and most problematic project (see Chapter 5). In Prince Edward Island townships gradually took root and Alexander Stewart, writing to his parents in 1805, was able to say unequivocally that life was better there than in Scotland. The Island continued to be a destination for emigrating Scots, particularly Highlanders from Skye and the Western Isles, although William Cobbett in 1830 was scathing. Commenting on the fact that 'sensible

Scots' were leaving Glasgow, he wrote, 'Those that are poor and cannot pay their passage, or can rake together only a trifle, are going to a rascally heap of sand, rock, and swamp, called Prince Edward Island.' Clearly, this was not a deterrent, and in fact by this time the Island had a viable economy, dominated by timber. In 1991 an exhibition at the Charlottetown Museum stated that Prince Edward Island was the most Scottish of all Canadian provinces.

At the same time as Scots were starting new lives in Prince Edward Island, across the Northumberland Strait another Scottish settlement was taking shape on the mainland. The arrival of the *Hector* at Pictou in September 1773 is often seen as initiating organised Scottish emigration to Canada, although John Macdonald of Glenaladale had taken his Highlanders to Prince Edward Island the previous year. But the voyage of the *Hector* has taken on a mythic resonance almost comparable to that of the *Mayflower* which took disaffected Puritans to New England. The *Hector* left the Clyde for Loch Broom on 5 June, in order to pick up emigrating families mainly from Wester Ross, Sutherland and Inverness-shire. The venture was the result of the partnership of two Scots, Dr John Witherspoon, a minister who had left Paisley in 1768 to go to New Jersey, and John Pagan, a Glasgow-based merchant and shipowner. The Philadelphia Company had acquired land grants along the Gulf of St Lawrence and was struggling to settle them. Witherspoon and Pagan joined the company and set about a vigorous recruitment campaign. Their agent in Ross-shire, John Ross, brought together the families who were to embark at Loch Broom.

It was July before the *Hector* set sail from Loch Broom. Three years earlier she had taken 200 emigrants to Boston, but she was an elderly ship and not in good shape. Her timbers were rotten and conditions were cramped and airless, providing a perfect breeding ground for disease. It wasn't long before dysentery struck and smallpox broke out. Eighteen of the seventy or so children on board, and several adults, died on the voyage. Storms added a miserable two weeks to the crossing and food supplies almost ran out. By the time they disembarked at Pictou the season was too far advanced for the weakened and demoralised settlers to prepare themselves for winter.

The emigrants had been told that there was already an established township at Pictou and that houses and provisions would be ready for them. It was true that they were not the first Europeans to arrive, or even the first Scots, but what greeted them was a densely forested wilderness scattered with a few rough cabins. 'Township' did not mean town. The most accessible land had already been taken. Several individuals and families drifted away to join more established communities where they could find work. Others spent that first harsh winter in primitive lean-tos. Local Mi'kmaqs helped them with gifts of food and showed them how to make and use snowshoes, absolutely essential for winter mobility. When the spring came, they were faced with the daunting prospect of felling trees, building log cabins and breaking the ground to plant their first crops. Most had never seen so many trees before in their lives and had never wielded an axe. Existing settlers, mainly Americans who had moved north and a group from Ulster (many of both originally from Scotland), showed them how. Others would follow the *Hector* vanguard. In 1801 the *Dove* and the *Sarah* arrived from Inverness with around 550 emigrants who had been cleared from Strathglass near Beauly. They had been recruited by Hugh Dunoon who needed to settle his Pictou land. In the same year the *Hope* sailed from Loch Broom with another hundred.

In 1786 when the Reverend James MacGregor from Perthshire arrived by canoe at Pictou Harbour he was somewhat dismayed. He, too, had been led to expect a town but found, thirteen years after the *Hector*'s arrival, acres of woods 'with here and there a mean timber hut visible in a small clearing'. MacGregor had responded to Pictou's request for a Presbyterian minister. He was twenty-seven years old when he arrived and spent the rest of his life there. His parish was widely scattered, and in the early years he travelled around it by canoe and on snowshoes, and shared the often frugal rations and meagre living conditions of his parishioners.

Although when James MacGregor arrived Pictou did not yet exist as a town, for ten years timber had been exported from the harbour and this was to prove the basis of its success. Timber was Nova Scotia's most prolific resource, but it did not become a major export until Napoleon's blockade of the Baltic ports in 1807. The Baltic countries were traditionally the source of the timber required in Scotland for shipbuilding, house construction, and other industries. When this source dried up, Nova Scotia, New Brunswick and Lower Canada were able to fill the gap. The timber ships delivered their cargo to ports all over Britain, and were conspicuous in the Clyde. Whenever possible they travelled back to North America with a human cargo. Many of the agents active in recruiting emigrants in the early decades of the nineteenth century were operating on behalf of timber merchants, who were themselves often shipbuilders, for example the Duthies of Aberdeen.

Scots were quick to recognise the commercial opportunities offered by North America, and they dominated the Canadian timber trade. Halifax and Pictou, and Miramichi in New Brunswick were key ports. The trade employed large numbers in the sawmills that were set up and as loggers, this being an important source of wages for emigrant families struggling to make newly-cleared land productive. One of the most enterprising figures in Miramichi was William Davidson from Inverness who with John Cort from Aberdeen in 1765 took up a 100,000 acre land grant on the Miramichi River and brought out settlers from Scotland. He was among the first to see the potential of timber and began to supply masts for the British navy. He also developed salmon fishing for export.

These commercial ventures took the merchants themselves from

Scotland to British North America, and they employed staff at the Canadian end of their businesses. William Loch after five years as an apprentice clerk in Edinburgh went to Halifax in 1816 and found employment with Messrs James Fraser and Co. James Fraser, from Inverness, was a major player in the timber trade. After a year Loch was sent to Miramichi where he became principal clerk, before setting up his own timber business.

Halifax had begun its existence as a military base, opening to civilian settlement in 1749. In the mid-eighteenth century it was a ramshackle and insanitary collection of wooden buildings occupied by soldiers, fishermen, traders who had moved north from New England, and a few settlers. By 1751 there were over 5,000 residents. Some of the disaffected Scots from Pictou and Prince Edward Island drifted south to Halifax, where they were more likely to get some form of employment. There was a need, according to an advertisement in the *Aberdeen Journal* in July 1784, for skilled tradesmen such as masons, carpenters and blacksmiths, as well as housemaids, which indicates a growing middle class. Nearly two hundred years later in his essay 'Portrait of a City' Hugh MacLennan described Halifax, where he spent his childhood, as having her face 'towards Europe; her back (which is the city dump) greets strangers from the continent. The smells of tar, fish-meal, bilge, ozone, salt water, spruce forests and her own slums are rich in her nostrils.' The smells were probably much the same, if more intense, when the town was in its early stages of development. For many emigrant Scots in the heyday of Nova Scotia settlement it provided their first experience of North America. Some got no further.

Halifax became the main British army and naval centre in North America with the evacuation of British troops from Boston in 1776, and it was to Halifax that around 30,000 Loyalist troops and refugees were shipped at the end of the American War of Independence. The influx doubled the population of Nova Scotia.

The rudimentary town could barely shelter and provide for them. They were housed in a variety of makeshift quarters – warehouses, sheds, churches, some in tents – while efforts were made to arrange more permanent settlement. This involved making 2.5 million acres available, some of which were recovered from unsettled grants. As much of it was obviously unproductive, there was good reason for this land being overlooked for settlement. In a lengthy, complicated and at times chaotic process land was allocated, mainly along the southeast coast and the Northumberland Strait as well as in what became the province of New Brunswick in 1784, and Prince Edward Island. Among the disbanded troops were the Royal Highland Emigrants, raised to fight the rebels in the American War of Independence. The regiment had been added to by new emigrants pressured to enlist when their ships were boarded before reaching Boston. Their families were sent to Halifax where they were cared for by the army for the duration of the war. It also included troops raised in North Carolina by Captain Allan Macdonald of Kingsburgh, husband of Flora Macdonald, celebrated for the part she played in assisting the escape of Charles Edward Stewart after Culloden. They, eventually, returned to Scotland.

Not all the disbanded soldiers were Scots, but very significant numbers of those who took up land grants were, and contributed to the Scottish character of many communities. They contributed also to attracting more Scots, particularly Highlanders, who were more likely to accept departure if they knew they were joining their own folk. Loyalists settled not only in Nova Scotia and New Brunswick. In 1759 General Wolfe had captured Quebec City from the French. Scottish troops had played a key role, in particular Fraser's Highlanders and a former Jacobite, Donald Macdonald, who had acquired fluent French while in exile which got him past the French sentries. For the remainder of the war, Scots were present in Quebec as administrators and merchants. The first governor was a Scot, James Murray, the general who had taken over from Wolfe after his death on the Heights of Abraham (named for Abraham Martin, Champlain's pilot up the St Lawrence) at the taking of Quebec City. One of the places settled by Fraser's Highlanders was Murray Bay on the north shore of the St Lawrence.

The New Brunswick and Nova Scotia Company, formed in 1831, acquired 550,000 acres in York County north of the Bay of Fundy, and recruited settlers in the West Highlands. The company's main concern was to secure a labour force for the timber industry and various inducements were used. They claimed to have spent three years and £80,000 on preparing for settlement. But it was a bad experience for the settlers, which began before they even left Scotland when they found that the promised free passage was not forthcoming. They left the Clyde in September, very late in the year, and the crossing took forty-three days. It was November before the emigrants reached their lots, where they had been told a log house awaited each family, with 5 acres of land cleared and planted. All they found were huts and inadequate provisions. In 1838, thirty-three families from Skye told their tale in a petition to the New Brunswick assembly in which they asked for assistance, saying that forty of their number had died and the rest were destitute. The families were eventually allocated Crown land.

The lower reaches of the St Lawrence had long been farmed by the French. In order to weaken French resistance Wolfe ordered his troops to destroy their farms. With the end of the war the government was anxious to consolidate the British presence and encouraged disbanded soldiers to settle. Some remained in Lower Canada, which would become the province of Quebec. When the Revolutionary War broke out in 1775 Loyalist refugees began to trek north from New York and New England, and after 1783 several thousand disbanded troops joined them. Now it was important to strengthen the border with the United States. Highland Scots were seen as ideal material to occupy a buffer zone on the Lower Canada border, the Eastern Townships, and former members of Highland regiments were offered land grants there, as well as on the Gaspé Peninsula in the north. Others took up grants further up the St Lawrence near Lake Ontario. The size of the grant depended on rank. Private soldiers received 100 acres, captains 700, field officers 1,000. Transport to the new territory was provided, and tools and basic provisioning to help the settlers to get started.

The Eastern Townships continued to attract Highland settlers. The British American Land Company, formed in 1833, had agents in the Highlands recruiting families to settle the 850,000 acres it acquired in the area. The first contingent of sixty families arrived in 1838. It included fifteen families cleared from the Seaforth estates in Lewis. Mackenzie of Seaforth was struggling to maintain his estates, and six years later they were sold to James Matheson whose policy was to encourage and aid emigration. In the 1850s hundreds left and made their way to Canada; the many Lewis placenames in the area bear witness to this connection. Although many of the Highlanders were virtually destitute when they arrived, over the years they built up a strong Gaelic community, centred mainly in Winslow Township. They farmed, fished, worked in forestry and road and railway building. But there was from the beginning a temptation to cross the border into the US in search of better wages and perhaps a less demanding existence. By the 1870s the migration south and also west to the Canadian prairies was diluting the Scottish character of the area. The First World War was another blow. Large numbers of young men from Scottish Canadian families joined the forces, leaving farms without the manpower to keep them going. Many of the vacated farms were taken over by French Canadians.

Farming was the expectation of most of those who came to the Eastern Townships and settlement followed the pattern that was becoming familiar to all the new communities in British North America. Where tracts of land were not acquired by individuals or land companies, they were administered by the Crown. Often they were inadequately surveyed or not surveyed at all, and land grant boundaries could be vague. This opened the way for squatters. It also explains the practice of 'singing the survey', where boundaries were paced out according to the number of times the 23rd Psalm was sung. For all settlers there followed what John Buchan described in his novel *Sick Heart River* (1941) as 'a pretty serious fight with nature'. The land had to be cleared and the felled trees used to build and furnish a log cabin. Potatoes and turnips were usually the first crops planted, utilising the space between the tree stumps. Many travellers commented on the ugliness of the stumps which remained, black and resistant, for years after the trees themselves were felled and disposed of. Another season of backbreaking work might enable the sowing of oats and wheat. Hunting and fishing supplemented the diet and provided deerskin for clothes and moccasins. Surplus timber could be sold, though it meant floating it downriver to the nearest sawmill. Gradually more land was cleared and cultivated. It was a gruelling existence, and it was often years before a farm was properly established, during which time a poor harvest or an unusually severe winter could be devastating. Not everyone was confident of survival, let alone success. 'We've turned into Indians right enough,' wrote one Gaelic poet; 'in the gloom of the forest none of us will be left alive, with wolves and beasts howling in every cranny. We're ruined since we left King George.'

The trials of pioneer life were highlighted in some of the material that was being published back in Scotland. Intense cold, often hunger, physical toil, and disappointed hopes all featured. But there were other factors, too, to do with re-forging an identity. Patrick M'Robert from Drumlanrig in Galloway produced his *Tour through Part of the North Provinces of America* in 1776. He wrote, 'everything is strange; you have all to seek, and as it were, to begin a world a-new; to acquire acquaintances; to struggle hard for a character etc. These require courage and resolution in the adventurer.' This sense of beginning with a clean slate could be both daunting and inspirational. It was easier for those who migrated and settled as a group, as many Scots did, retaining existing relationships and traditions. For them the crucial factor was the survival of the community, and co-operative effort and mutual support were what saw them through. Nevertheless, expectations were often unreal and often dashed.

The pioneering settler who cleared the forest and built a home and a community consolidated the British colonial presence, yet government policy on emigration was ambivalent. Soldiers, especially Highland soldiers who were still regarded with a degree of circumspection, could well be planted to hold the frontier, but the drainage of human and financial resources out of the mother country was not to be encouraged. Commercial exploitation, however, was something else. Scottish merchants were quick to benefit when peace came to North America in 1763. They traded from mainly Clyde ports and from Aberdeen and Leith, and soon had agencies established in Nova Scotia, New Brunswick and on the St Lawrence. By 1770 there were at least eleven firms based in Glasgow and Greenock trading to Quebec. In 1805 fifty-eight firms in Greenock, Glasgow, Port Glasgow and Saltcoats in Ayrshire sent ships to Halifax. Timber was the main cargo brought back; rum, bibles, gunpowder, tools and materials for shipbuilding and maintenance, as well as people, went out. Between 1760 and 1825 there were 279 businesses and shipowners operating in the Canada trade, including the transport of emigrants. The traffic was a boost to shipping and shipbuilding, and the many trades which contributed to both. It affected a wide constituency of those whom it employed – the shipwrights, the sailors, dockers, agents and clerks on both sides of the Atlantic. To maintain activities in Canada required supplies as well as skills, and many of the necessary products were made in Scotland. The Carron Iron Works near Falkirk did very well out of exporting cast iron – pipes, engine cylinders, domestic stoves, agricultural and domestic implements – to North America. Much of it was made from American pig iron. Growing communities meant an increase in demand for household commodities also, many of which – domestic pottery, for example – were supplied by Scottish manufacturers.

British North America was inevitably occupying a larger space in Scottish consciousness, and not only because people were leaving to go there. At an early stage its commercial potential was identified. The *Glasgow Journal* in January 1760 described it as 'a source of trade and commerce' and as an outlet providing 'constant consumption for all our goods, products and manufactures'. Two weeks later the same journal returned to the theme with a liberal sprinkling of exclamation marks. 'An exclusive fishery! A boundless territory! The fur trade engrossed! And innumerable tribes of savages contributing to the consumption of our staple! – these are sources of exhaustless wealth!'

By this time the North American fur trade had been pursued for nearly a century. The involvement began officially with the formation in 1670 of the Company of Adventurers and the designation Rupert's Land for the vast area beyond the St Lawrence and the Great Lakes that was granted to the Company. This territory, challenged at times by the French, became the domain of the Hudson's Bay Company, as it was soon called, for two hundred years. The Company would have a massive role in the North American story, and Scots would have a massive role in the Company. Operations were run from London and Moose Factory, the first fort constructed on Hudson Bay in 1672. But there were also fur traders and trappers operating independently and in 1768 Montreal merchants were formally allowed to engage in the fur trade, although not in Rupert's Land which remained Hudson's Bay Company territory. Out of this was born, in 1779, the North West Company. It was operated from Montreal, by Scots. The man with a controlling interest in the North West Company was

Simon McTavish, the son of a lieutenant in Fraser's Highlanders who had taken part in the successful attack on Louisbourg in 1758. Simon was born around 1750 in Stratherrick, near Inverness, and went out to the American colonies in 1763. He got involved in the fur trade in Albany on the Hudson River, and then in Detroit. In 1775 he went to Montreal, gravitating to a centre of fur trading action and also escaping the American war. He quickly established himself as a major player, and within a few years he was a leading light in the dominant group of mainly Highland businessmen and bankers who laid a very Scottish foundation for Montreal's commercial development.

The building on that foundation, in a literal sense, would be seen in the next century when the mansions and business premises of Scottish financiers, merchants, company directors, railway developers and lawyers made their conspicuous imprint on the city. Even after another century Hugh MacLennan could say, in his book *Rivers of Canada* (1974): 'So many of these had high-coloured Scottish faces that an Edinburgh man confided to me that he felt more at home in Montreal than he ever felt in Glasgow.' The Montreal-based Scottish network was a financial and political force. Another of the fur-trading clan was James McGill from Glasgow, born in 1744 and in Montreal by the time he was twenty-two years old. Like most of those who rose to the top of the fur trade, he did his training in the field. He would become a member of the assembly of Lower Canada, and give his name to the university he endowed. The Scottish network remained a force to be reckoned with through the nineteenth century, when it provided a Tory bulwark against radical agitation, in which Scots also took a lead. The legacy of Scottish prominence in Montreal is still in evidence, in institutions, buildings and street names, over two hundred years after it took hold.

The network extended beyond Montreal and beyond Scotland. William Forsyth, for example, was based in Halifax where he set up as a general merchant in 1784. Before long he was shipping fish and timber not only to Britain, but also the Caribbean and the United States, where his agents were Scots, thus maintaining an exclusively Scottish commercial web. In 1788 he won a seven-year contract to supply the British navy with masts. The Patterson brothers, who with Edward Mortimer from Keith in Banffshire helped to make Pictou the commercial centre of the Gulf of St Lawrence, were trading to Jamaica. Allan Gilmour, a Scottish-based timber merchant operating out of Grangemouth on the Forth initially, then Port Glasgow on the Clyde, opened branches at Miramichi and Quebec City. In 1830 the firm exported 300 shiploads of timber.

The business muscle of Scots was more than a matter of commercial benefit for Britain and profits for individuals. It made it possible for more Scots to join the enterprise. The network was a focus of recruitment; family and personal connections counted for a great deal. The ambience of energetic success which surrounded Scottish commercial activities in Montreal proved highly attractive. This was the other side of the dispossessed Highland settler coin. Many of the Scottish business tyros were also from the Highlands. They were determined, adventurous, courageous, but they were not about building communities. In fact, they were suspicious of settlement. The source of their profits was wilderness, and although they had markets in the new countries of the Caribbean and the United States as well as the old country, British North America was more important as a resource than as a market. They needed a labour force that would exploit that resource without destroying the environment that nourished it. They were pioneers in a different sense from those who felled the forests to make space for homes, farms and families.

In 1791 the territory on either side of the St Lawrence below Montreal was designated Lower Canada, while that to the south and west became Upper Canada. In 1784 Cape Breton Island and

New Brunswick became separate provinces. Government was by provincial assembly, which operated with relatively little interference from London. Scottish business clout ensured that the political role of Scots was also considerable. But as the new century was entered, the extensive territory that was British North America was still only thinly settled: pockets of the maritime provinces, a narrow strip along the St Lawrence, the outpost of Lower Canada's Eastern Townships. With the defeat of Napoleon in 1815 there was a new wave of emigration which filled many of the spaces and propelled settlement westward.

The end of the war brought economic hardship to communities all over Scotland. Wages fell, disbanded soldiers swelled the ranks of those without work, and radical agitation made the authorities nervous. In the Highlands, increasing numbers of landowners were encouraging or forcing their tenants to leave. In the Lowlands, where the pace of industrialisation had outrun social and civic infrastructures, thousands were dispossessed and disaffected. Official resistance to emigration weakened. The majority of those who departed from Scotland in the first half of the nineteenth century went to British North America.

The traffic across the Atlantic was constant. The sparsely populated settlements in Nova Scotia and Prince Edward Island grew as mainly Highlanders, displaced or desperate and often both, joined existing communities and founded new ones. Some arrived bewildered, sometimes ill-nourished or sick, with few possessions and no money, putting an enormous strain on the meagre resources of existing settlements. The best land was quickly taken up, and the later arrivals often found themselves struggling against wilderness resistant to the plough to feed their families. Only about a quarter of Cape Breton was amenable to agriculture. Many Highlanders found that 'new Scotland' was all too similar to the barren, rocky acres generations had struggled to cultivate in old Scotland. Along the coast and on the shores of the extensive Bras d'Or lake system, a crucial occupation was fishing, as was the case for many Hebridean and Highland coastal communities who no longer had land for crops or beasts.

New arrivals disembarked at Quebec, at Pictou, at Charlottetown in Prince Edward Island, at Sydney in Cape Breton, at Saint John and Miramichi in New Brunswick, at Halifax. In 1817 the *Hope* and the *William Tell* brought nearly 400 people from Barra to Sydney and the *Elizabeth* made two sailings to Saint John with passengers from Dumfries. In 1819 the *Economy* sailed to Pictou with nearly 300 passengers taken on from the island of Colonsay and Tobermory in Mull and the *Morning Field* picked up nearly 200 at Tobermory and Glenelg, bound for Quebec. From 1816 to 1821 the *Good Intent* left Aberdeen each spring bound for Halifax, Pictou or Miramichi. Over the same period the *Harmony* sailed regularly from Greenock and Aberdeen to Halifax, Pictou and Miramichi. Between 1820 and 1825 the *Monarch* made seven sailings from Leith to Miramichi. In 1819 Alexander Allan of Saltcoats sailed from Greenock to Quebec and as a result founded the Allan Line which made regular sailings to British North America. This is just a snapshot; over the summer season, from April to August, the movement of people and goods across the Atlantic never ceased, with some ships making two sailings in a season.

Settlement spread from Pictou and from the growing community further east at Antigonish (first settled in the 1790s by soldiers of disbanded Highland regiments), reaching inland when coastal land grants ran out. Antigonish attracted Catholic Highlanders and soon became a predominantly Catholic area. Tension between Protestant and Catholic, and between differing strains of Presbyterianism, travelled with the emigrants, although it was often some time before communities were able to recruit a minister or build a church. Not all were as open-minded as the Reverend James MacGregor who joined the Pictou community in 1786. 'I resolved not to confine my visitations to Presbyterians, but to include all of every denomination, who would make me welcome; for I viewed them as sheep without a shepherd.' The minister, when there was one, had a multi-stranded and highly stretched role. As well as performing the usual tasks of a parish priest, often over a wide and inhospitable area, he was called upon to act as schoolteacher, doctor, lawyer and general adviser where such professional skills were absent – and they generally were. Most settler communities were totally occupied with survival and were without the resources to pay the stipend of a minister or to employ a teacher for the children, but some support was available from the old country. In Glasgow in 1825 a society was formed to support the 'Religious Interests of Scottish Settlers in British North America' and three years later the Edinburgh Ladies' Association was founded which also helped to send ministers, as well as bibles, across the Atlantic.

As late as the 1870s some ministers were peripatetic, conducting open air communion services for numbers far too great to be accommodated indoors. People were hungry for the word of God. At Strathlorne in August 1872, for example, a congregation of a thousand attended an open air service for over five hours, two of them in the pouring rain. Education was equally problematic. Travelling schoolteachers were, like travelling ministers, quite common, in the early years likely to be poorly qualified and poorly paid. Legislation of 1811 provided support for free public schools, and in 1826 it became compulsory for all communities of over thirty families to set up schools, but as late as 1863 it was estimated that over 50,000 children were receiving no formal education.

Pioneering life made demands on children as well as adults, which ensured that even among Scots, who traditionally had a high regard for literacy and valued education as a route to a better life, schooling was a luxury. Many families could not afford to allow their children away from the work demanded by the homestead. But pioneering in Nova Scotia did not only encompass a life of rural toil which required input from every member of the family. By the end of the eighteenth century coal mining was being developed in Cape Breton, in the Sydney and Glace Bay areas. The mines employed not only new emigrants but those who were finding it difficult to survive on the land. In the thirty years from 1827 annual coal production grew from less than 12,000 tons to nearly 268,000 tons. By 1894 it had reached nearly a million tons, which more than tripled over the next eight years. Sydney itself, born when two Scots took up adjoining land grants in 1780, became a garrison town and port, was augmented by Loyalists, but did not receive its town charter until 1885.

The maritime provinces continued to receive Scots, particularly Highland Scots, and the influx of new blood from the old country helped to reinforce and sustain the Highland character of many areas of settlement. Families tended to join those from the old communities who had gone before. Ties of kith and kin remained powerful. Even as late as the twentieth century, many Scottish emigrants to Canada had never ventured beyond the boundaries of the island or parish of their birth before they boarded the ship that was to carry them across the Atlantic. They found awaiting them people, often of their own name, with a shared knowledge of place and tradition, and a shared language. In many ways it was easier to keep these alive in the new Scotland counties of Inverness, Antigonish or Pictou than in the old Scotland Lowland counties of Renfrew, Lanark or Dumbarton to which so many of their fellow Highlanders were migrating.

CHAPTER THREE

Men Fare Well Enough

Here men fare well enough, with fine prosperous homes,
something they would not see in their lifetime had they
remained on the other side.

HUGH MaCCORKINDALE

WHEN IN 1817 the Reverend William Bell arrived in Perth, he found a town of around a hundred buildings and was impressed by the fact that the streets were 'regularly laid out'. This was Perth on the River Tay. Not the river that flows out of Loch Tay to be joined by the Lyon and to wind on past Aberfeldy and the cathedral town of Dunkeld to another Perth and on to Dundee, but a new Perth at the heart of a 'Scotch settlement' that stretched for seven miles. This River Tay flowed into the Rideau, a tributary of the Ottawa River. The community had existed for two years and included a large number of discharged soldiers. Stirling, Bannockburn, Arnprior, Renfrew and Lanark on the River Clyde are not far away.

In 1856 an official pamphlet was published to promote Upper Canada as a destination for those thinking of emigrating from Britain. Upper Canada, now Ontario, spread west of the upper St Lawrence River, taking in the shores of Lakes Ontario, Erie, Huron and Superior, and stretching north to Hudson Bay. The story of Scottish settlement began with soldiers who fought in the French and Indian Wars and the Loyalist exodus from the Thirteen Colonies in the 1770s and '80s. Although many went to the Maritimes, a substantial number were encouraged to occupy the frontier area west of the St Lawrence. The author of the pamphlet, JM Grant, pointed out that British North America was the colony nearest to

Britain and therefore easier and cheaper to get to than Australia or New Zealand which had by this time entered the picture as emigrant destinations. He went on to say that Upper Canada had 'a healthy and bracing climate, a soil which produces all the crops usually raised in this country, land so cheap and so easily obtainable that every industrious man may become a freeholder'. Land was still being offered as the main enticement, and the assumption was that those who came to Canada would come as farmers, whatever their occupation in the old country.

Grant added to the list of attractions the fact that Canada's rivers and lakes provided 'an unsurpassed means of communication', and that there was 'a greater degree of security than can be enjoyed in any other British colony'. Most of those with experience of settlement in the eighty years or so since Scots first began to make their homes in Upper Canada would probably have wanted to qualify those statements, and some of them did. But throughout this period the possibilities offered by this part of British North America were attracting individuals and groups, and some parts in particular took on a distinctively Scottish character at an early stage.

One thing was unquestionable: the way in which settlement developed was determined by the waterways. It would have been more accurate if Grant had written that the rivers and lakes offered the only means of communication, since, as many dismayed settlers discovered, roads hardly existed and travelling on foot, horseback or by cart was difficult and slow. Settlement snaked out along the rivers: the St Lawrence, its major tributary the Ottawa and its tributaries, and the river systems that emptied into the lakes. These were lifelines, but the rivers themselves were also problematic as most of them had stretches that could not be navigated. Everyone heading from Montreal to Upper Canada had to bypass the Lachine rapids, which involved negotiating a rough stony track until something more like a road was built. For many this was their introduction to the nature of the land itself. By the 1820s canals and locks were being built to bypass rapids, link up waterways, and generally make river navigation easier.

The Loyalists who established themselves in Upper Canada came from the south. Many of them made their way from the Mohawk Valley, west of Albany on the Hudson River, where they had settled on land originally acquired by Sir William Johnson. Some were veterans of the French and Indian Wars. Johnson also brought in Highlanders from Inverness-shire and the west of Scotland in an effort to populate the very large territory he had acquired. A group of around 400, led by the tacksmen brothers Allan, Alexander and John MacDonell, sailed in August 1773 on the *Pearl* from Fort William at the head of Loch Linnhe to New York. There was an outbreak of smallpox on board, and twenty-five children died on the voyage. These were Catholic families, traditionally Jacobite supporters, who saw little future for themselves in Scotland. Their disillusion with Highland landlords at home may have contributed to their adherence to King George when the Thirteen Colonies rebelled. The Mohawk Valley, like other Highland communities in America, responded to the call for recruits for King George's American regiments.

Scotland's Glengarry lies north of Fort William, reaching west towards Knoydart, still one of the most wild and remote parts of the West Highlands. It was MacDonell country. When in 1784 the Mohawk Valley people made their way north they took the name with them, and where they settled along the upper St Lawrence River became Glengarry County. The Loyalist settlers were joined over the next few decades by friends and family, as Highland emigration intensified. They arrived in 1785 and 1786, the latter group a substantial migration of families evicted from Knoydart to make way for sheep. Upper Canada, they believed, would enable them to maintain a traditional Gaelic community. As was recognised at the time, this was not an isolated event. 'These people, when once they settle in Canada, will encourage others, as they are now encouraged by some friends before them. They will form a chain of emigration.' This is exactly what happened. More came in 1790. As the struggle for survival in Scotland's Glengarry intensified, a local priest, Alexander MacDonell, encouraged migration to factory jobs in Glasgow. When this source of livelihood also failed he came up with the idea of the Glengarry Fencibles (fencible regiments were raised to defend home territory), which saw service in Ireland, a Catholic regiment in action against Catholic Irish dissidents. In 1802 it was disbanded, leaving the men with no means of support. Alexander MacDonell conceived of a plan to enable them to emigrate to Upper Canada. He raised money from landowners and industrialists to pay their passage: 800 joined the Glengarry settlement. By 1806 there were over 10,000 Catholic Highlanders from Scotland's Glengarry area in Canada's Glengarry, and the exodus continued. 'Go not to Glengarry, if you're not a Highlandman,' commented John MacTaggart in an 1829 guide.

Whatever the difficulties and oppressive experiences they had left behind, the settlers were not prepared for the years of dispiritingly hard work required to establish a new life in Canada. Land had to be cleared and homes built. As in Nova Scotia, trees were seen as a formidable and threatening obstruction, although they were also a resource which provided not only the most widely used material for building but, as settlements became more established, a source of income. Often the toil of felling trees, shaping and transporting logs, and burning what could not be used, had to be followed by clearing stones before the land could be cultivated. It was an agonisingly slow process. In 1821, when the earliest Glengarry settlers had been in occupation for nearly forty years, the area still looked undeveloped, according to John Howison who passed through. He was, he said, disappointed, 'the improvements bearing no proportion to what I had anticipated'. He went on:

The majority of its inhabitants were indeed very poor when they commenced their labours, and had a variety of discouraging circumstances to contend with, the principal of which were, the peculiarities of the climate, the almost inaccessible situation of their farms, the badness of the roads, and the immense woods which encumber the soil. They have, in some degree, surmounted the greater number of these difficulties; but still the settlement is not in a very flourishing state, and its inhabitants seem too unambitious to profit by the advantages of their condition.

One measure of success was the length of time it took to 'upgrade' from log cabin to frame house. Most of the houses, John Howison commented, were still built of logs and contained only one apartment. This lack of progress was ascribed by Howison to the settlers having 'no inclination to improve their mode of life, being dirty, ignorant, and obstinate'. Although Howison makes no explicit reference here to Gaels, contemporary comment often compared Highland settlers unfavourably to the more industrious Lowlanders, echoing the not uncommon dismissal of Highlanders in Scotland as lazy and shiftless. Adam Fergusson, for example, commented on the 'less profitable traits which stamp the Highlander as more at home in wielding the claymore, or extracting the Highland dew, than in guiding the ploughshare to slow but certain results'.

Compared with the homes most of Glengarry's settlers had left behind, log cabins had much to recommend them. They were roughly fifteen feet by ten, and around eight feet high. The logs were notched at each end to fit together at the corners, and the chinks between them were filled with moss or ferns and plastered with mud. A slanted roof of poles was covered with bark or turf. Logs were split to make an even surface for flooring, and there was a stone hearth. The furniture was also made of logs. The cabins had to withstand the intense cold of winter, heavy snowfalls, lashing rain and the heat of summer. Building a log house was a skilled and generally communal task. A newly-arrived greenhorn family relied on the assistance of established settlers. It was imperative to construct some form of shelter very rapidly, however rudimentary. Sometimes a rough shanty went up in a day, to be replaced by a more substantial cabin once more trees had been felled and logs cut.

Ten years after John Howison, Adam Fergusson, an Edinburgh lawyer (quoted above), visited Upper Canada and was rather more impressed. 'Upper Canada appears to be blessed with all the solid materials of human happiness, independence and comfort,' he wrote in his *Practical Notes Made During a Tour in Canada* (1831). But many settlers' first reaction to wilderness was total dismay. John Galt describes it well in his novel *Lawrie Todd* (1830), which although set in the Mohawk Valley conveys the experience of many in Canada. Lawrie Todd and his family approach their 50-acre lot by a muddy track which is 'the mere blazed line of what was to be a road'. The work of felling has already begun. 'Hundreds on hundreds of vast and ponderous trees covering the ground for acres, like the mighty slain in a field of battle, all to be removed, yea, obliterated, before the solitary settler can raise a meal of potatoes, seemingly offer the most hopeless task which the industry of man can struggle with.' The first shanty is flooded out, the second consumed by a forest fire. Later in the novel he comments, 'the discomforts of the first few years of a new settlement are unspeakable'.

It was hardest, of course, for the pioneers but in places like Glengarry, where whole communities shared the experience and were subsequently strengthened by known new arrivals, such hardships were endurable. The Upper Canada land grants were not all fertile and it could take many years to make a farm productive. Drought and grasshopper plagues added to the difficulties of the Glengarry folk. 'We shall go to the land of contentment,' wrote

Anna Gillis from Morar, who sailed on the *Macdonald* from Greenock in 1786, bound for Glengarry County, and in another poem, 'landlords will no more oppress us'. Contentment may have taken time to achieve, but the Glengarry community not only survived, it retained its distinctively Highland character for many generations – indeed, still does. After half a century Fergusson was struck by the fact that 'the language, the customs, the native courage of their Celtic sires, still distinguish the clan', although he did not overlook the negative aspects of Highlanders preserving their old habits.

A century and more later Ralph Connor was writing novels set in Glengarry which evoke a more benign environment although they do not downplay the pioneering experience. In *Glengarry School Days* (1902) he describes life in Twentieth, the 'twentieth section' of the settlement. The children make their way home from school along a road that runs

> ... through the deep forest of great pines, with underbrush of balsam and spruce and silver-birch; but from this main road ran little blazed paths that led to the farm clearings... Here and there, set in their massive frames of dark green forest, lay the little farms, the tiny fenced fields surrounding the little log houses and barns.

There is still a sense of the vulnerability of human habitation but the hard work and community values that taming the forest required are celebrated. Connor writes of the 'brittle Highland courage toughened to endurance by [the Highlanders'] long fight with the forest, and with a self-respect born of victory over nature's grimmest of terrors'. It is Buchan's 'serious fight with nature' again.

Much further south, on Lake St Clair between Lake Huron and Lake Erie, Lord Selkirk made another attempt at settlement, a scheme he had initiated before being diverted by the possibilities of Prince Edward Island. He acquired a land grant of 1,200 acres which he named Baldoon after his own estate in Kirkcudbrightshire, and brought around a hundred Highlanders to settle on it. Although Selkirk put considerable effort into planning the settlement, arranging for homes to be ready for the new arrivals and crops planted, it was not a success. The emigrants had a difficult voyage and reached Baldoon to find the houses not yet ready. Heavy rains washed out both the tents in which they had to be accommodated and the newly-planted crops. The land was swampy and malaria-ridden. Within the first year there were several deaths, and others abandoned their land grants. The man whom Selkirk had appointed to oversee the settlement, another Alexander MacDonell, proved inept and extravagant – he had diverted resources into the construction of a fine house for himself. A further setback was the invasion by the Americans in 1812. By 1817 only a handful of settlers remained.

At around the same time as Baldoon was failing to get established, an Irishman called Colonel Thomas Talbot was acquiring land to the east, along the north shore of Lake Erie. He expressed a preference for Englishmen, but the twenty-eight townships which he obtained were settled by large numbers of Scottish Highlanders as well as by Americans tempted by the prospect of land, although they were to find that outright ownership was not part of Talbot's plan. The Scots came mainly from Argyll and Perthshire. Talbot, like so many others, promised more than he delivered and wielded an autocratic control over the settlement which by 1832 was home to nearly 30,000 people. Colonel Talbot is memorably described by JK Galbraith, whose antecedents emigrated to Upper Canada from the shore of Loch Fyne in Argyll. Talbot, he writes, 'was Irish, aristocratic, eccentric, irreligious, and often drunk, and he was in possession of land that the Scotch believed they should own'. They did eventually succeed in buying it.

After the 1812 war with the United States Lord Bathurst, the

British colonial secretary, devised a plan to settle ex-soldiers and civilians in the strategic area along the upper St Lawrence. Government policy was still to discourage emigration, but the reinforcement of a bulwark against British North America's southern neighbour was felt to be important. The Bathurst Plan was a way of both controlling emigration and strengthening British territory. The plan was to provide government support for those already intending to emigrate who agreed to go to what became known as the Rideau Settlement, named for the Rideau River which flowed north into the Ottawa. Emigrants were offered free passage and land grants of 100 acres. Heads of families had to pay a deposit of £16, plus £2 for a wife, which was repayable after two years at the settlement. The deposit was to discourage people from abandoning their land and crossing the border into the United States. In spite of this many did leave, although over the years the area attracted large numbers of Scots.

Discharged soldiers were the first to settle there and in the eyes of some the half-pay officers in particular had undue influence. The initial response from Britain was not as great as Bathurst had hoped, although most of the 700 who elected to take up the offer were Scots. Sailing from Greenock in the *Atlas*, the *Baptiste Merchant* and the *Dorothy* they arrived in Quebec in September 1815, not a good time of year to begin life in Upper Canada. They had to spend their first winter in barracks in the existing settlements of Prescott and Brockville, at government expense, before continuing on their way the following April. According to William Bell, who joined the settlement in 1817, each settler was supplied with a spade, adze, felling axe, brush-hook, bill-hook, scythe, reaping-hook, pitch-fork, pick-axe, nine harrow teeth, two hoes, hammer, plane, chisel, auger, handsaw, two gimlets, two files, one pair of hinges, one door, lock and key, nine panes of glass, one pound of putty, fourteen pounds of nails, a camp kettle and frying pan, and a blanket for each adult and for every two children.

Crosscut saws, grindstones and sledge hammers were shared. The list gives a good picture of the work that faced the settlers and the way they would live.

William Bell's son Andrew in a letter of 1819 echoed the reaction of many from Scotland who arrived in the Maritimes and Upper Canada, whether shaped by misinformation or wishful thinking: 'When we left home, we thought the land would be covered with grass, and only a few trees here and there. But how great was our disappointment, when we found the ground was all covered with large trees.' Nevertheless, he believed the arduous labour required to clear and cultivate the land was worthwhile as it was ultimately productive: 'we raise wheat, potatoes, Indian corn, buck wheat, pumpkins, melons, cucumbers, and a great many kinds of French beans, besides all the kinds of things you have at home'. His father, like many others, reiterated that anyone averse to hard work should not contemplate leaving Scotland for Canada.

The main town was named Perth and the tributary of the Rideau on which it sat became the Tay. When Bell arrived to take up his appointment as minister he found a town of about thirty log houses in streets 'regularly laid out', but he considered the settlement to be badly run and failing to realise its potential. Crop yields were poor with little surplus to bring in cash with which to purchase goods. Bell's view was that an injection of capital and industry was needed:

> Could a few gentlemen, possessing spirit and capital, be persuaded to establish manufactories in this settlement, they would tend greatly to promote the prosperity of the colony... Labour, provisions, and building materials, are both cheap and abundant, and mechanics of all descriptions can be readily obtained.

Bell himself energetically set about his duties, covering many miles on foot and by canoe to preach to scattered communities and improvising premises for services. Sometimes the congregation was far too large to be accommodated under one roof and Bell would preach in the open air to the assembled crowd, who listened with their saddled horses tethered beside them. Bell's view was that Upper Canada had a long way to go before it deserved the 'flattering accounts' which were current. These, he said, 'were more like descriptions of what it may be fifty or a hundred years hence, than of what it is at the present time'. He went on: 'This province possesses great natural resources, and, I have no doubt, will at some future time support a dense population; but immense improvements must be made, and many years pass away before this takes place.'

By the 1820s the Lowland emigration societies were being organised and ships were departing from the Clyde filled with redundant handloom weavers and other skilled artisans. Some were destined for Upper Canada, and Lanark near Perth was a name indicative of Lowland settlement. The *Greenock Advertiser* commented on one departure in May 1821.

> The emigrants, generally, have a most respectable appearance; and amongst them are various artificers, such as smiths, joiners, etc, whose labours in their respective occupations must prove peculiarly valuable to the other settlers in their agricultural operations, to which the whole purpose to devote themselves under the encouragements held out by the Government, whose bounty, we are well persuaded, has in few instances been more judiciously bestowed.

Whatever the need for the skills they brought with them, most of these people were taking up land grants and would become farmers in conditions quite unlike anything they had known in Scotland. Some, at least, seemed to adapt well. 'I am very pleased to handle the axe, instead of the shuttle, and would not, for a good deal give up my present for my past employment,' wrote Robert Lamond in an account of the experiences of emigrants from Lanark and Renfrew.

In spite of discouragement and experiences for which the emigrants were quite unprepared, this part of Upper Canada continued to attract more Scots, and new settlements were being founded in other areas. Between 1815 and 1821 about 4,000 arrived to settle Bathurst in the Ottawa valley. William Dickson of Dumfries founded Dumfries township west of the western end of Lake Ontario. The township included the village of Galt, named after John Galt the novelist, a friend of Dickson. Dickson had originally emigrated to the United States, and the first settlers of Dumfries were from New York State. They walked into Upper Canada. Dickson also recruited families from Roxburghshire and Selkirkshire in the Scottish Borders. Within twenty years or so there were about 6,000 inhabitants of the settlement.

John Galt's association with Canada was more than the naming of a town by an admirer. His interest began when he represented Canadians seeking reparation for property damaged in the 1812 war and continued when he became secretary of the Canada Company, founded in 1824 and chartered two years later. The aim of the company was to acquire and settle land in Canada, and it successfully negotiated for over a million acres in the area between Lake Huron and Lake Ontario, the Huron Tract. A condition was that the company brought people and development to this vast area. It was a tall order, especially as the preference was for emigrants of some substance, which weighted recruitment against Highlanders, who as clearances intensified tended to be of meagre resources, if not destitute.

In 1825 Galt went to Upper Canada himself as one of a commission of five sent to investigate the territory the company was planning to buy. Two years later he was in Canada again, and with fellow Scots set off north from the village named after him in order to select a site for a new town, to be called Guelph. Having made their choice they symbolically felled a maple tree, taking turns with the axe. 'The tree fell with a crash of accumulating thunder, as if ancient Nature were alarmed at the entrance of social man into her innocent solitudes with his sorrows, his follies and his crimes.' Galt's comment in his autobiography suggests a not entirely optimistic vision of Guelph's future, but in fact the account that follows is upbeat:

> The works and the roads soon drew from all parts a greater influx of inhabitants than was expected, insomuch as the rise of the town far surpassed my hopes...mills projected have been built, a respectable bridge constructed, several taverns and a ball-room, and as a mark of the improved society, there are, I have heard, several harps and piano- fortes in the town. It was with me a matter of design to give a superior character to the place, and therefore although the first settlers were not of that rank of life to make such things important, I encouraged dances and public associations among them.

For Galt, taming the wilderness was not just about chopping down trees. However, his enthusiasm for spending on infrastructure was considered rashly extravagant and he was relieved of his post. And although Guelph itself flourished, with a population of nearly 2,000 by 1837, in ten years only half of the Canada Company's million acres had been taken up.

John Galt's novel, *Bogle Corbet, or, The Emigrants* (1831), is much more than a narrative of pioneering experiences, in the West Indies as well as Canada. He explicitly intended it as a guide. 'The object of this work,' he wrote in the preface, 'has been to give expression to the probable feelings of a character upon whom the commercial circumstances of the age have had their natural effect, and to show what a person of ordinarily genteel habits has really to expect in emigrating to Canada.' He went on to say that the novel 'contains instruction that may help to lighten the anxieties of those whom taste or fortune prompts to quit their native land, and to seek in the wilderness new objects of industry, enterprise, and care.' It is clear that part of Galt's purpose was to encourage people of means and education to settle in Canada, without underplaying the hardship that was involved. One of his characters offers the advice that the frontier is for the young: 'At your time of life, the hardships of the woods are no' wholesome, nor new ways an easy conquest.' For older people, who might find 'the awesome solitude of the wild woods, and the wanchancy neighbourhood of bears and bees' too much, an established town was a better proposition. Towards the end of the novel Galt reiterated his message:

> The man must indeed be strangely constituted, who above fifty emigrates for life, with habits and notions of the old country rivetted upon him, and yet expects to meet with aught much better than discomfort. Emigration should be undertaken at that period when youths are commonly sent to trades and professions: the hardships are too heavy an apprenticeship for manhood and to riper years penalty and privation.

Galt also interjected stinging criticism of the authorities' failure to run the colony appropriately and to handle immigration adequately:

> Canada, and indeed all the colonies, are a burden on the British people greater than need be. I do not, however, ascribe the fault to them but to the negligent colonial system of the mother country – if system it can be called, which is

literally no more than the sending of troops to keep possession, and of making a few civil appointments for the sake of patronage... Yearly, thousands on thousands of emigrants arrive at Quebec; but such is the void of all arrangement, that these helpless shoals of British subjects are left to shift for themselves, and to wander up and down, as if the very apparatus of the state had been instituted only for the behoof of those who fill official situations.

He pointed out that there was no official source of information on lands open for settlement, no maps, and no consistent policy of support and back-up. He suggested a scheme to enable settlers to pay for land grants by working on public projects, such as road building. New arrivals were often dependent on anecdote and happenstance for information. Galt advised that they should always seek out those with local knowledge and experience.

The very lack of system Galt criticised allowed his company and many others to acquire often vast stretches of land as a speculative venture and without fully worked-out plans. Although Galt's message in *Bogle Corbet* is that frontier life is hard, the Canada Company was itself criticised for mis-selling its product. Patrick Bell, born near Scotland's Perth and inventor of the reaping machine, emigrated to Upper Canada in 1834 and was blunt about the experience: 'They held out great prospects to Emigrants at home and coaxed and flattered every one that thought of coming to this Country...'. Those who 'swallowed the bait' then found themselves in thrall to the company and without promised amenities – non-existent roads, bridges and mills unbuilt: 'produce dwindled to one half of what was held out while the necessaries of life that they required to purchase were double what they expected. The settlers on the large Huron tract were last winter literally starving and in a state of open rebellion against their cruel seducers.' Bell himself returned to Scotland after four years.

Galt probably genuinely believed he could combine profit with benevolence. Others made no pretence of disguising their motives. Archibald MacNab left Killin in Perthshire in 1822, escaping creditors. He went to Upper Canada and acquired a land grant on the Ottawa River which became MacNab Township, with Arnprior as its main town. In 1825 he brought in around a hundred of his clansmen, to whom he had lent money for their transatlantic passage and onward journey. Along with the people, he transplanted a grotesque version of clan feudalism, forcing them not only to pay him in kind for their loans and land holdings but to hand over a proportion of their crop yields in perpetuity. While MacNab built himself a fine house and became a justice of the peace and politically influential, the township's settlers struggled against unmitigated odds with no support, constantly undermined by MacNab himself. He claimed the timber they felled as his own to sell: nothing, in fact, according to MacNab, belonged to the settlers, who were virtual serfs. MacNab's authority and influence were such that he was able to quell objections and convince the colonial government that all was well. It was not until 1840 that an official investigation revealed the true state of affairs and provided compensation for the exploited settlers. But they had had fifteen years of misery, only gradually discovering that MacNab's regime was not the normal experience of settlement.

The vast distances and poor communications meant that it was hard to detect the activities of the unscrupulous or criminal. Land allocation could be haphazard at the best of times, and a government keen to have particular areas settled did not ask too many questions. There were those who deliberately took advantage of this. One such was Donald Cameron who fraudulently claimed to have fulfilled his obligation of placing settlers on his Upper Canada land grant. The colonial government caught up with him. The Durham Report, which came in 1838 in response to political upheaval in Canada, gave a picture of Upper Canada which showed that after half a century of steady settlement much of it was still undeveloped frontier country. 'A very considerable portion of the Province,' it stated, 'has neither roads, post offices, mills, schools, nor churches.' With some exceptions, 'all seems waste and desolate; a widely scattered population, poor and apparently unenterprising, though hardy and industrious... living in mean houses, drawing little more than a rude subsistence from ill-cultivated land'.

Susanna Moodie would have recognised this description. She and her husband John, an Orkneyman who had served as an officer in the Napoleonic Wars, sailed from Leith in July 1832 on a nine-week voyage to Quebec. They were cabin passengers. Also on board were seventy-two steerage passengers, who ran out of food two weeks before arrival. Fortunately, the captain was in a position – and of a mind – to help them out from the ship's stores. They were heading for an existing farm near Cobourg on Lake Ontario, not a new land grant, but after a short time moved on to a new grant near to Susanna's sister at Lake Katchawanook near Peterborough. Their brother Samuel Strickland had emigrated some time earlier, and after three years as an officer of the Canada Company at Guelph and Goderich had settled in that area. The Moodies named the farm Melsetter, after a village on the Orkney island of Hoy.

The Moodies were a middle-class family. They found life hard and the work demanding. They ran out of money and could not afford hired labour, so Susanna had to help her husband with the field work. 'I had a hard struggle with my pride before I would consent to render the least assistance on the farm, but reflection convinced me that I was wrong – that Providence had placed me in a situation where I was called upon to work – that it was not only my duty to obey that call, but to exert myself to the utmost to assist my husband, and help maintain my family.' She had to learn skills that she never imagined she would need and accept circumstances which she found not only difficult but sometimes offensive.

Susanna Moodie wrote about her experiences, and her *Roughing it in the Bush* (1852) and *Life in the Clearings versus the Bush* (1853) are among the best-known accounts of pioneer life in Canada. Like Galt's *Bogle Corbet, Roughing it in the Bush* was written in order to instruct intending emigrants. Her bluntest warning comes at the end. Life in the backwoods may be fine for 'the poor, industrious working man' but for 'the poor gentleman' there is nothing to recommend it:

> The former works hard, puts up with coarse, scanty fare, and submits, with a good grace, to hardships that would kill a domesticated animal at home. Thus he becomes independent, inasmuch as the land that he has cleared finds him in the common necessaries of life; but it seldom, if ever, in remote situations, accomplishes more than this. The gentleman can neither work so hard, live so coarsely, nor endure so many privations as his poorer but more fortunate neighbour. Unaccustomed to manual labour, his services are not of a nature to secure for him a profitable return. The task is new to him, he knows not how to perform it well; and, conscious of his deficiency, he expends his little means in hiring labour, which his bush-farm can never repay. Difficulties increase, debts grow upon him, he struggles in vain to extricate himself, and finally sees his family sink into hopeless ruin.

She modified these views in her second book, and the Moodies themselves did not sink into hopeless ruin. John Moodie was eventually appointed sheriff of Hastings Country and they left their farm to live in nearby Belleville. Susanna Moodie may have been constrained by class and a comfortable upbringing in Suffolk but she was not blinkered, and there is a refreshing honesty in her approach. She ends *Roughing it in the Bush* by saying, 'If these sketches should prove the means of deterring one family from sinking their property, and shipwrecking all their hopes, by going to reside in the backwoods of Canada, I shall consider myself amply repaid for revealing the secrets of the prison house, and feel that I have not toiled and suffered in the wilderness in vain.' Her message is clear: emigration is for the working classes.

Susanna's sister Catherine Parr Traill, who was the author of books for children and wrote *The Young Emigrants* (1826) before she had experienced emigration herself, also married an Orkneyman, John Moodie's friend and fellow-officer Thomas Traill. They, too, went to Upper Canada. Several books followed, and like her sister her aim was to instruct. Although she emphasises that the frontier experience is not for the faint-hearted and is particularly challenging for the middle classes her tone is much more positive than her sister's. In both her practical guides and her stories for children she celebrates frontier skills. In *Lost in the Backwoods: A Tale of the Canadian Forest* (1882), she shows the children of a former Highland soldier married to a French Canadian re-enacting the pioneer experience as they fend for themselves in the wild. They build a log house, make furniture, hunt for food, make clothes and moccasins from animal skins and utensils out of bone. Friendship with a Native girl teaches them new skills – Catherine Parr Traill is a wonderful example of nineteenth-century political correctness. She underlines the moral of the tale: 'The Canadian settler, following in the steps of the old Americans, learns to supply all his wants by the exercise of his own energy. He brings up his family to rely upon their own resources, instead of depending upon his neighbours.' Nevertheless, the value of collective effort and co-operation is equally part of the message.

Like Galt, Traill steps out of her narrative to comment. Here is her description of a 'bee', the coming together of a community to build a house or a barn, or to fell and clear an area of forest.

A Bee is a practical instance of duty to a neighbour. We fear it is peculiar to Canada, although deserving of imitation in all Christian colonies. When any work which requires many hands is in the course of performance, as the building of log-houses, barns, or shanties, all the neighbours are summoned, and give their best assistance in the construction. Of course the assisted party is liable to be called upon by the community in turn, to repay in kind the help he has received.

Her sister's view of the same activity is rather different. In Susanna's eyes logging bees are 'noisy, riotous, drunken meetings, often terminating in violent quarrels, sometimes even in bloodshed'. In her introduction she makes specific reference to what she considers rose-tinted misrepresentations of the activity to be found in material published for emigrants. Pamphlets 'talk of log houses to be raised in a single day, by the generous exertions of friends and neighbours, but they never ventured upon a picture of the disgusting scenes of riot and low debauchery exhibited during the raising, or a description of the dwellings when raised – dens of dirt and misery'. Catherine is less fastidious, and seems to relish the endless tasks that are part of frontier life. *The Female Emigrant's Guide and Hints on Canadian Housekeeping* (1854) is packed with practical advice and the constant theme is that of hard work. 'In Canada persevering energy and industry, with sobriety, will overcome all obstacles,' she states briskly. And: 'In this country honest industry always commands respect: by it we can in time raise ourselves, and no one can keep us down.' If Susanna despairs at the 'dens of dirt and misery', Catherine determinedly demonstrates how even in the roughest circumstances standards can be maintained.

Her message is, of course, aimed mainly at women. 'The giants of the forest are not brought down without much severe toil,' she writes, 'and many hardships must be endured in a backwoodsman's life, especially by the wife and children.' She then proceeds with methodical common sense to outline what is required, beginning with the natural resources on hand to be exploited. Timber provides material for houses, sheds, barns, fencing, furniture and firewood, with the bark used for making baskets and mats and ashes for fertiliser and soap. Maple trees provide syrup, and she tells us how to collect and process it. Dyes can be obtained from plants, and there is abundant wild food. Coffee can be made from dandelions and tea from sassafras. There are recipes for venison, squirrel, hare, wild duck and geese, and fish. She tells us how to make soap and candles. The raising of sheep and cattle brings another round of tasks: shearing the sheep, spinning, dying, weaving and knitting; and milking, cheese and butter making. There are instructions on how to establish a garden, raise poultry, and make bread and rag rugs. There is also information and advice on the best way to cross the Atlantic, fares, timetables of steamers and trains once in Canada, currency, wages and postage.

Between them, the two sisters give a memorable picture of what settlement life was like in Upper Canada in the 1830s and '40s. Susanna, in spite of the unambiguous nature of the warning she sounds, in fact conveys much that is positive, and underlying Catherine's upbeat pragmatism there is a somewhat daunting emphasis on the relentless nature of the tasks involved. It is perhaps not surprising that when the opportunity arose sobriety was conspicuous by its absence. Not all those who settled Upper Canada in the first half of the nineteenth century stuck it out. Some moved off the land, as the Moodie family did. Some moved west, especially after 1885 when the railway made prairie settlement feasible. Many were tempted across the border to the United States. The Scottish tradition of mobility did not end with the crossing of the Atlantic. But large numbers did stay where they first put down Canadian roots, and many communities remained distinctively Scottish.

JK Galbraith, in his 'memoir of the clansmen in Canada' (first published as *Made to Last* in 1964, reprinted in 1967 as *The Non-potable Scotch*), describes the area where he grew up in the 1920s and '30s, the area on the north shore of Lake Erie which had once been the Talbot Townships. It is liberally scattered with Scottish names although they are attached to the smaller places rather than the towns. He lists Iona, Wallacetown, Campbellton, Fingal, Crinan, Glencoe, Port Bruce and Cowal, some of these actual places in the Highlands, others altered or invented. Scottish family names were even more prominent. 'Not even in the Western Isles are the Scotch to be found in more concentrated solution,' he writes, and mentions McPhails, Grahams, McFarlanes, McKellers, McKillops, Camerons, Morrisons, Gows, Galbraiths, McCallums, Pattersons and McLeods, mainly, though not all, Highland names. His description of these communities demonstrates that their Scottish – or Scotch, the designation he prefers – nature was expressed in much more than names.

Galbraith supplies a kind of afterword on the tribulations reflected in the books of Susanna Moodie and Catherine Parr Traill. The communities that are the subject of his book, while not spectacularly successful, had survived, and he pays tribute to what that survival entailed:

Once the Scotch must have displayed a phenomenal capacity for innovation and adaptation in their farming methods. The transition from the spare, wet, and treeless crofts of the Highlands and the Western Isles to the lush forests, deep soil and strong seasons of the land by the Lake could scarcely have been more dramatic. It is true that they had always lived in intimate association with their cattle and sheep; to understand these in Scotland was to understand them in Ontario. But the soils, crops, crop rotation, the insects and plant diseases, the problems of farm architecture, machinery and drainage, even the wagon that went to town, were all different. Within a matter of a few months men made the transition from an agricultural system in which they were guided by the experience of centuries to one where a very great deal depended on a man's capacity to figure things out for himself or imitate with discrimination those who could.

Not everyone could claim with Hugh MacCorkindale, who went to Upper Canada from Islay, that emigration had brought them 'fine prosperous homes', but most would probably have agreed that men, and women, fared 'well enough'. 'It was a lucky day for many Highlanders when they sailed over here,' MacCorkindale wrote.

CHAPTER FOUR

A Kind of Kingdom by Itself

*The Hudson's Bay is not an ordinary commercial
company, but a kind of kingdom by itself...*
JOHN BUCHAN

AS SETTLEMENT SPREAD along the rivers and lake shores of British
North America, a vast territory to the north and west was inhabited
and traversed by the First Nations tribes and a few hundred
employees of an organisation that had an extraordinary impact on
Canada's history. Although founded in London and run from there,
the Hudson's Bay Company was dominated by Scots. So was the
North West Company, which emerged when groups of independent
fur traders amalgamated in 1779. Twenty years later there were over
1,200 Nor'Westers in the fur trade, three-quarters of them operating
west of Grand Portage on Lake Superior, south of present-day
Thunder Bay. They included Scots, French and Métis. The North
West Company was controlled from Montreal, and those in charge
were Scottish Highlanders. In 1821 the North West Company and
the Hudson's Bay Company merged.

The extraordinary success of the fur trade depended on the
demand in Europe particularly for beaver pelts which were made
into the highly fashionable beaver hats. It also depended on the
vigour and stamina of the traders and the co-operation of the
Native peoples who trapped the animals. The traders travelled
thousands of miles, mainly on water, taking trade goods in one
direction and furs in the other. For the Nor'Westers, operating
out of Montreal, it could take two years to complete a trip. The

Hudson's Bay Company bases in the Bay, Moose Factory, York Factory and Fort Churchill, shortened the distances but gave less ready access to good waterways. Gradually both companies built a network of trading posts. By 1821 the HBC had seventy-six and the NWC ninety-seven, but every fur still had to be brought back for shipment across the Atlantic.

The story of the fur trade runs in counterpoint to the story of settlement, although some of the challenges and the skills required were the same. For the Scots, settlement was predominantly a family, and often a community, affair, and the wish to preserve a threatened way of life was sometimes a motive for abandoning the old country. The life demanded by the fur trade was different from anything most Scots who joined it had ever experienced, but it soon became apparent that Highlanders and Orkneymen had qualities admirably suited to the rigours of wilderness survival. They were the same qualities that put Scots in the forefront of exploring and charting that wilderness.

Rupert's Land, the territory designated with the founding of the Hudson's Bay Company in 1670, was a territory of 1.5 million square miles, encompassing the north of present-day Ontario and Quebec, Manitoba, Saskatchewan and Alberta, a large chunk of the Northwest Territories and part of Minnesota and North Dakota. It was known to be thinly populated by Native groups and densely populated by beaver. The French had made some tentative incursions, and in the century that followed individuals pushed further north and west in their quest for furs, but it was the 1780s before serious and organised attempts were made to explore the territory. The Treaty of Paris of 1783 excluded British fur traders from the newly created United States of America, which particularly affected the Nor'Westers who had traditionally operated further south than the Bay Company. This was the spur to looking elsewhere, not only for furs but to find out if there was a sea route through the Arctic to the west which would both open up new markets and enable easier shipment back to Europe.

At the end of the eighteenth century of the two rival fur-trading companies the Nor'Westers had the upper hand. At their head was Simon McTavish, the most conspicuous of a troop of larger-than-life characters. He was thirteen when he left the Scottish Highlands for the American colonies and an apprenticeship in the fur trade. By the 1780s he had a controlling interest in the North West Company and was presiding over an extraordinary lifestyle. An emblem of this lifestyle was the Beaver Club, founded in 1785 in Montreal. Membership was limited to fur traders who had proved themselves in the wilderness; only those who had spent at least one full season upcountry, in *le pays en haut*, could join. As if to compensate for the rigours, privations and loneliness of life in the wilderness the Beaver Club was the epitome of conviviality and excess. It was also seen as being typically Highland, although it was an experience that most Highlanders would never encounter. Huge amounts of food and drink, raucous songs and war whoops, dancing on the table, broken crockery and ultimate drunken collapse were the hallmarks of the meetings. On one occasion the twelve members present consumed 120 bottles of wine in addition to ale, porter, gin and brandy. The talent for high living wasn't confined to Montreal. When the Nor'Wester nabobs made their progress to the annual rendezvous at Grand Portage (after 1783 at Fort William, as the former fell on the US side of the border), they did things in style. Washington Irving described the scene:

> They ascended the rivers in great state. They were wrapped in rich furs, their huge canoes freighted with every convenience and luxury, and manned by Canadian voyageurs, as obedient as Highland clansmen. They carried up with them cooks and bakers, together with delicacies of every kind, and an abundance of choice wines for the banquets which attended this great convocation.

This was a level of luxury to which most Highland chieftains could not aspire and a universe away from the lifestyle of the growing numbers of Highlanders who were struggling to make their homes in the infant settlements.

Another leading Nor'Wester was Alexander Mackenzie, born in Stornoway in 1764. Like McTavish, he went to the American colonies as a child, but at the age of fifteen he was sent to Montreal to join a counting house run by John Gregory, whose partner James Finlay was a fur trading pioneer, probably the first Briton to reach the Saskatchewan Valley from Montreal. After five years in Montreal, Mackenzie was eager to get out into the field and he quickly proved himself to be a skilled trader. Like many of the Scottish fur traders, Mackenzie combined a keen business sense with a single-minded courage that could be ruthless. In 1789 he set out on a journey that took him from Fort Chipewyan on the western shore of Lake Athabasca to the Arctic Ocean, down the river that would be named after him. He explained his thinking in his own account of the journey:

> I was led, at an early period of life, by commercial views, to the country Northwest of Lake Superior, in North America, and being endowed by Nature with an inquisitive mind and enterprising spirit; possessing also a constitution and frame of body equal to the most arduous undertakings, and being familiar with toilsome exertions in the prosecution of mercantile pursuits, I not only contemplated the practicability of penetrating across the continent of America, but was confident in the qualifications, as I was animated by the desire, to undertake the perilous enterprise.

This blend of curiosity, adventurousness and confidence is found in many of the Scots who imprinted the development of Canada. Although this first attempt proved not to be the route through to the Pacific, four years later Mackenzie made the journey across the Rockies that led him to the Pacific shore, although without discovering the legendary Northwest Passage. Commenting in his book *Scotchman's Return* (1960), Hugh MacLennan enlarges on Mackenzie's self-portrait:

> ... only a man from a country as lonely and ghost-ridden as the Highlands could have the insane determination to paddle a canoe through the Rocky Mountains and down La Grande Rivière-en-bas to the Beaufort Sea, and that nothing was more in the life-style of the Highlander than Alexander Mackenzie's feat in searching for the Northwest Passage in a canoe. After an achievement of incredible boldness and endurance, what, after all, did the Highlander find but nothing?

Mackenzie's journeys may not have yielded what was being sought, but they did add greatly to knowledge of the vast hinterland that was so crucial a commercial resource. Mackenzie and his companions travelled by canoe and by foot. They struggled through fiercely hostile terrain and weather conditions, often on the move for eighteen hours at a time and with food supplies scarce. They were a necessary vanguard of the continuing drive to the west. Another great river was put on the map by Simon Fraser, born in Vermont of Scottish Loyalist parents. He too moved north and by 1801 was a partner in the North West Company. In 1805 he was building trading posts along the Peace and Parsnip Rivers, which had been Mackenzie's route west. Three years later he made his way down the river that was to be named the Fraser.

Recruitment for both the NWC and the HBC was through a combination of contacts and tradition. Personal recommendation and family connections counted for a great deal. When Simon McTavish died in 1804 he was succeeded by his nephew William MacGillivray, who was not the only member of the McTavish extended family to join the company. The Hudson's Bay Company had for many decades a preference for Orkneymen, who from the 1740s were recruited annually when the company's supply ships called at Stromness to take in fresh water and provisions before crossing the Atlantic. In the eighteenth century over three-quarters of the HBC payroll were from Orkney, and until 1891, when the HBC ships stopped calling at Stromness, the link between Orkney and Canada was maintained. Although many of the Orkneymen eventually returned to Orkney, some bringing home with them Native or mixed-blood wives and families, others lived out their lives in British North America. It was often their union with 'country wives', as they were called, that kept them there, although some of the children of these unions were sent to Scotland to be educated. The legacy of the Orkney connection was expressed in the Orkney Homecoming which took place in 1999. It brought hundreds of descendants of Orcadians to the islands.

The Orkneymen were preferred because they were considered adaptable, self-sufficient and unassuming. Murdoch Mackenzie, writing about Orkney in 1750, commented that the people of Orkney were healthy and hardy and 'capable of an abstemious and laborious life': they probably didn't have much choice. The English explorer Samuel Hearne described them as 'the quietest servants and the best adapted for this country [Canada] that can be procured'. But their quietness and clannish mutual support overlaid what he called 'slyness' and a 'propensity to smuggling, and clandestine dealings of every kind'. George Simpson, who became overseas governor of the Hudson's Bay Company in 1826, preferred Highlanders, but then he was a Highlander himself. One Scottish employee of the HBC who was neither a Highlander nor an Orkneyman was Robert Ballantyne, who subsequently became a best-selling writer of adventure stories. Ballantyne joined the Company as an apprentice clerk in 1841. He arrived at York Factory and then had to make his way west to Lake Winnipeg. One of the first things he learned was that river travel did not always mean sticking to the water. All the rivers used by the traders and voyageurs had rapids and waterfalls which could only be negotiated by portages. Sometimes the boats themselves were carried. Sometimes their contents were carried while the boats were hauled through the rapids, which is what Ballantyne describes here, in his memoir *Hudson's Bay, or Every-day Life in the Wilds of North America* (1859):

> Some of the men, jumping ashore, ran briskly to and fro with enormous burdens on their backs; whilst others hauled and pulled the heavy boats slowly up the cataract, halooing and shouting all the time, as if they wished to drown the thundering noise of the water, which boiled and hissed furiously around the rocks on which we stood.

The men were accustomed to carrying two 90 lb loads at a time, sometimes three, clambering over rocks and cutting their way through dense undergrowth.

Rupert's Land, says the trapper hero of Ballantyne's novel, *Away in the Wilderness, or Life among the Red Indians and Fur-Traders of North America* (1879), was 'nothing but lakes, and rivers, and woods, and plains without end, and a few Indians here and there, with plenty of wild beasts everywhere'. There were trading posts 'scattered here and there, from the Atlantic to the Pacific, and from Canada [i.e. what is now Quebec and Ontario] to Frozen Sea, standin' solitary-like in the midst of the wilderness, as if they had dropped down from the clouds by mistake and didn't know exactly what to do with themselves'. This was the territory that was familiar to the hundreds of Scots who worked in a whole variety of capacities for the HBC. Some travelled thousands of miles to trade with the Native peoples who actually trapped the beaver and prepared the skins; others were recruited as factors, to man the factories or trading posts; or as the clerks, carpenters, masons and surgeons who had to supervise supplies, keep the books, maintain premises, equipment and people in circumstances dominated by extremes of weather and distance, and often by privation.

Scots were seen as having the self-sufficiency and determination that the enterprise required, at every level. They were physically tough, used to rigorous terrain and climate, although nothing in Scotland could fully prepare them for the demands of the Canadian north. They were also mentally and morally tough, schooled, many of them, in the unforgiving classrooms of Calvinism. This emerged in the ethos of the Hudson's Bay Company which, in contrast to the more exuberant Nor'Westers, has been described by one historian of the Company, Peter Newman, as 'parsimonious paternalism'. The HBC ran a tight ship, although this did not mean that those at the top were unfamiliar with the rewards of success. They knew how to lead expansive lives.

But for most of the Company's employees, expansive was a word applied to the territory they covered rather than the lives they led, and for others, particularly the few women, life was severely constricted. The letters of Letitia Hargrave, married to James Hargrave, chief factor at York Factory, give a picture of a community making the best of a limited existence. Letitia was from Campbeltown in Kintyre, and her brothers William and Dugald McTavish were both employed by the Hudson's Bay Company. It was through them that she met James Hargrave, born in Hawick in the Borders. At York Factory the little community endured 'nine months of winter varied by three months of rain and mosquitoes'. Winter meant being snow and ice bound: 'Our ink gets frozen and is bad,' Letitia wrote, 'there will be none better till the ship comes – the Madeira in the store is still solid. They can't fill the wine kegs till the barrelsfull thaw – the oil is in the same state.' As this suggests, domestic life was a strange combination of extremes – the climate, food shortages, disease – and the maintaining of middle-class standards, with servants, table silver, crystal and good wine. The high points were the arrival of the Hudson's Bay Company ships after the ice had broken up, bringing supplies, letters from home, and perhaps new blood to enliven the community.

For the son of an Orkney tenant farmer or a Highland crofter, employment with the HBC offered both adventure and security – of a kind. It also offered a hard and more often than not dangerous life. Robert Campbell is an example of a Highlander who responded to the challenge. He left Glen Lyon in Perthshire to join the Hudson's Bay Company. In 1834 he was posted to the Mackenzie River country and in 1856, after twenty-two years of gruelling and often lonely labour, became chief trader at Fort Chipewyan on Lake Athabasca. After another eleven years he became chief factor. He not only ran the trading post, he explored into the northwest, setting up the first HBC trading post in the Yukon and discovering the source of the Pelly River. (There is a mountain called Glenlyon Peak beside the Pelly.) In 1848 he established Fort Selkirk, originally Campbell's Fort, where the Pelly joins the Yukon. In 1859 he married Eleanora Stirling, having returned to Scotland to find a bride. He spent his latter years ranching at Elphinstone in northwest Manitoba.

In a lecture to the Historical and Scientific Society of Manitoba in 1898, four years after Robert Campbell's death, the Reverend Dr Bryce paid tribute to his qualities.

Robert Campbell was a natural leader of men. His tall commanding figure, sedate bearing, and yet shrewd and adaptable manner, singled him out as one of the remarkable class of men who in the service of the Hudson's Bay Company governed an empire by their personal magnetism, and held many thousands of Natives in check by their honesty, tact, and firmness.

There were others like Campbell, who provided the backbone of the HBC network, but the real governor of the Company, in name and deed, was George Simpson. Simpson grew up in Dingwall, Easter Ross, and joined the Hudson's Bay Company in 1820 at the age of twenty-four, after an apprenticeship with a London sugar company. Six years later he presided over the whole of the HBC's territory. He was autocratic, determined and ruthlessly pragmatic. Although he could not rival his North West Company predecessors, he travelled in style, proceeding by canoe – with piper, Colin Fraser from Sutherland, advertising his progress. One contemporary, John McLean, an HBC chief trader, was succinctly critical of the Simpson rule. 'In no colony subject to the British Crown is there to be found an authority so despotic as is at this day exercised in the mercantile colony of Rupert's Land,' he wrote, and went on: 'an authority combining the despotism of military rule with the strict surveillance and mean parsimony of the avaricious trader. From Labrador to Nootka Sound [on the west coast of Vancouver Island] the unchecked, uncontrolled will of a single individual gives law to the land.'

Simpson was ambitious for himself and for the company, and travelled extensively as part of the effort to expand the fur trade and exploit commercial possibilities. In the interests of both, he championed exploration and the search for the Northwest Passage, a primary theme in nineteenth-century exploration. He also encouraged his traders to collect material for the newly-opened Museum of Science and Art (now part of the National Museums of Scotland) in Edinburgh. This came about through his friendship with Daniel Wilson, professor at the young University of Toronto and brother of the museum's first director George Wilson who was keen to collect native North American material. Who better to collect it than the HBC employees whose work brought them into close association with the Native peoples and their ways of life? Robert Campbell was one of several who sent Native artefacts and natural history specimens to the museum. Another was James

Hargrave from Hawick, who from 1840 was in charge of York Factory on Hudson Bay before moving to Sault Ste Marie. Roderick McFarlane from Stornoway, who was with the company for over forty years, latterly in charge of the Athabasca district, was the most prolific collector of material for dispatch to Edinburgh. The Bay Company connection contributed to the National Museums of Scotland now having one of the most important collections of aboriginal North American material in Britain. It remains a very tangible link with Canada.

If beaver led Scots across the Atlantic to explore the land, whales led them to explore the Arctic seas. By the middle of the nineteenth century Peterhead was Britain's main whaling port and Scottish whalers were among the first to penetrate Arctic waters. They, like the HBC supply ships, called at Stromness in Orkney, and Orkneymen made their contribution on the ocean frontier as well as the land. Whaling was hazardous in the best of conditions. In the Arctic huge risks were taken to capture whales before the ice returned at the end of the brief summer season. With an increasing demand for whale oil, used in Dundee's expanding jute industry, and whale bone (baleen) which provided the main material for the corsets worn by most Victorian women, greater risks were taken and the whaling ships ventured further west and north. The whaling captains were at the forefront of a new wave of interest in the Arctic and the possibility of a Northwest Passage through to the Pacific. William Penny, for example, master of the *Bon Accord* out of Aberdeen, in 1840 rediscovered Cumberland Sound, unvisited by a European for 250 years. During his whaling voyages Captain Penny made notes on ice and weather and the sounds and inlets of Baffin Island.

The first state-sponsored voyage of Arctic exploration had occurred twenty-two years earlier, when John Ross, son of a Church of Scotland minister, entered Lancaster Sound with the *Isabella* and the *Alexander*, only to turn back because he believed its exit was closed by mountains. His nephew James Ross accompanied him, and took part in a second expedition the following year under William Parry, which sailed right through the sound. John and James Ross sailed again in 1829. They were ice bound, presumed dead, and it was four years before they were eventually picked up by a whaler in Lancaster Sound. During that time they had made several important overland journeys and James reached the Magnetic Pole, before an extraordinary voyage in small boats took them to safety.

Less well known than the Rosses are John Richardson and John Rae, both remarkable men who made valuable contributions to knowledge of the Canadian Arctic. Richardson, from Dumfries, studied medicine at Edinburgh and became a naval surgeon in 1807. In 1819 he joined the first expedition led by John Franklin, with the objective of exploring the Arctic coast. The journey took them overland to Lake Athabasca, then north to Great Slave Lake, and on to the coast. Winter caught them with provisions low and their canoes damaged and unusable. They headed inland on a desperate journey in savage weather during which ten of the party died of starvation and one was shot by a Native guide, who in turn was despatched by Richardson. The rest survived by eating lichen scraped from trees and boiled shreds of animal skins. Without Richardson it is likely that more would have died. He rallied the weak, attended to the sick and collected food and fuel, and all the time never lost sight of his scientific role, collecting and recording specimens and making observations.

Richardson was a key figure in Franklin's second expedition in 1825, which also included Thomas Drummond from Midlothian, a botanist described by Richardson as 'the most indefatigable collector of specimens'. Drummond later explored in the Rocky Mountains and collected specimens for Glasgow's Botanic Gardens. Richardson himself was a modest man, and down-played his achievement though not the challenge:

Coronach in the Backwoods by George Simson, 1859.
A Highland family in newly cleared Canadian forest keep their music
alive in the midst of homesickness.
(Trustees of the National Museums of Scotland)

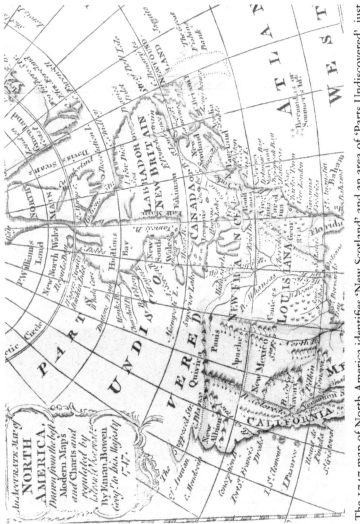

The 1747 map of North America identifies 'New Scotland' and an area of 'Parts Undiscovered', just before Scots began to settle in significant numbers.

(From *The Romance of Commerce*, 1907)

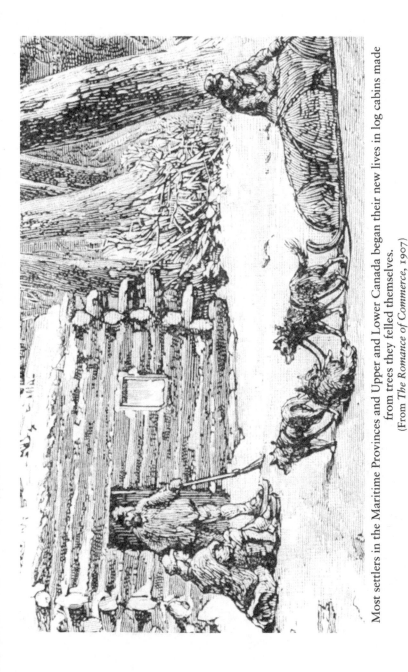

Most settlers in the Maritime Provinces and Upper and Lower Canada began their new lives in log cabins made from trees they felled themselves.

(From *The Romance of Commerce*, 1907)

Quebec City. Many immigrants arrived at Quebec, having sailed up the St Lawrence. Most continued their journey upriver to Montreal and then on to their final destinations.
(From *The Romance of Commerce*, 1907)

Junction of the Ottawa and St Lawrence rivers. Rivers and lakes were the main highways for immigrants.
(From *Canadian Scenery Illustrated* by WH Bartlett, 1842)

Brockville on the upper St Lawrence was a staging post for many travelling to settlements in Upper Canada. (From *Canadian Scenery Illustrated* by WH Bartlett, 1842)

It could take years to clear sufficient land to create a productive farm.
('First Settlement'. From *Canadian Scenery Illustrated* by WH Bartlett, 1842)

Trappers on the Churchill River. Trappers and fur traders were the vanguard in opening up the wilderness.
(From *The Romance of Commerce*, 1907)

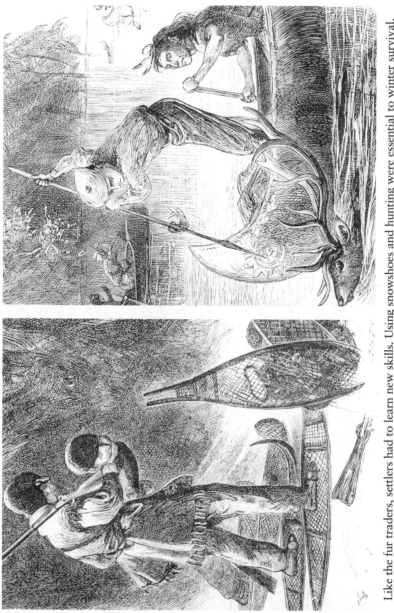

Like the fur traders, settlers had to learn new skills. Using snowshoes and hunting were essential to winter survival.
(From *The Young Fur Traders*, 1856, by RM Ballantyne)

Toronto attracted many Scots, and became a focus of radical ideas and political activity.
(From *Canadian Scenery Illustrated* by WH Bartlett, 1842)

The Canadian Pacific Railway in the Rocky Mountains.
(From *The Romance of Commerce*, 1907)

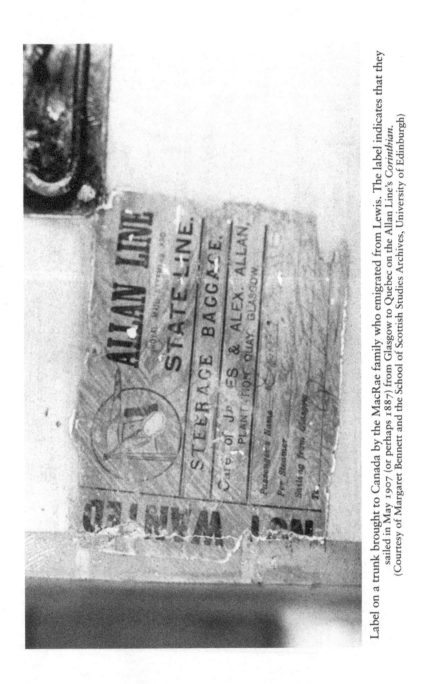

Label on a trunk brought to Canada by the MacRae family who emigrated from Lewis. The label indicates that they sailed in May 1907 (or perhaps 1887) from Glasgow to Quebec on the Allan Line's *Corinthian*. (Courtesy of Margaret Bennett and the School of Scottish Studies Archives, University of Edinburgh)

Angus Morrison at Marsboro, Eastern Townships, with a family photograph showing his grandparents, his mother and his aunt, who emigrated from Harris in the early 1880s.
(Courtesy of Margaret Bennett and the School of Scottish Studies Archives, University of Edinburgh)

John D MacLeod at Whitton in the Eastern Townships. In 1850, he left
Lewis with his parents as a child of six or seven.
(Courtesy of Margaret Bennett and the School of Scottish Studies Archives,
University of Edinburgh)

A poster advertising the Scottish steamship company the Allan Line, enticing would-be emigrants with promises of assisted passage, free land grants and good wages.

Pipers at the opening ceremony of the 55th Fergus Scottish Festival and
Highland Games in Ontario.
(Lynn Boland Richardson)

I had to travel over a country reaching from the great American lakes to the islands of the Arctic Sea, and embracing more than a fourth of the distance from the equator to the pole, which had never before been visited by a professed naturalist. I perceived at once the magnitude of the field, and comprehended at a glance that it was far beyond my grasp… but I thought I could at least record what I saw; and I determined to do so as intelligently as I could and without exaggeration, hoping in this way to furnish facts on which the leaders of science might reason, and thus promote the progress of Natural History to the extent of my limited ability.

When in 1845 John Franklin embarked on another Arctic expedition, Richardson was not with him. But three years later he was back on the Arctic coast. Franklin and his party had vanished, and Richardson, with an employee of the Hudson's Bay Company called John Rae, was looking for them. The following year Richardson, by now in his fifties, returned to England, leaving Rae to carry on the search. It was not until spring 1854 that Rae learnt from passing Inuit news of what happened to Franklin.

Rae was from Orkney, born near Stromness. Like Richardson, he had studied medicine at Edinburgh and in 1833 was appointed surgeon to the Hudson's Bay Company. Initially based at Moose Factory, he quickly demonstrated a keenness to get to grips with the environment and to refine existing skills and learn new ones – hunting, sledging, using snowshoes, canoeing. He had a talent for improvisation and experiment, and understood the value of native survival skills, which he adopted himself. He also had a talent for dry understatement. His comment on plunging waist deep into freezing water in order to recover a canoe was 'there being no handy opportunity of changing clothes or drying myself, (it was freezing pretty hard), I was not quite comfortable'. On another occasion, when the temperature was forty degrees below freezing, he remarked 'some few degrees more heat would have been preferable'. Rae was identified by Sir George Simpson as a man who could pursue the company's aim 'to complete the geography of the northern shore of America', and he duly set off in July 1846 to Repulse Bay, just within the Arctic Circle. It was the start of fifteen months of surveying in extreme conditions which saw every member of the party return in good health except for some frostbite and considerable loss of weight.

On this and subsequent journeys Rae's strategy was to travel light, and rely on hunting for food to avoid being weighed down by provisions. (The Franklin party had been carrying tinned meat, which may have contributed to their downfall, both through its weight and bulk and the fact that it may have been tainted.) He had extraordinary stamina and commitment, and an unusual readiness to learn from the Native peoples who had adapted so successfully to an unforgiving environment. One of his first teachers was a Cree called George Rivers. His respect for ways of life that were often at that time considered uncivilised, or even degenerate, proved offensive to the British establishment and contributed to its reluctance to believe Rae when he reported evidence of cannibalism among the beleaguered Franklin party. Something of his character and methods is conveyed by this description of Rae from RM Ballantyne's book about his time with the Hudson's Bay Company:

He was very muscular and active, full of animal spirits, and had a fine intellectual countenance. He was considered, by those who knew him well, to be one of the best snowshoe walkers in the service, was also an excellent rifle shot, and could stand an immense amount of fatigue... He does not proceed as other expeditions have done – namely, with large supplies of provisions and ten or twelve men... The party are to depend almost entirely on their guns for provisions... and penetrate into these unexplored regions on foot.

Rae covered more Arctic miles than any previous white explorer and travelled faster. When Sir George Simpson asked him to take on the 1846 expedition he wrote, 'As regards the management of people and endurance of toil, either in walking, boating or starving, I think you are better adapted for this work than most of the gentlemen with whom I am acquainted.' It was not Simpson's style to pull punches when outlining what Rae was likely to experience.

The Hudson's Bay Company initiated several expeditions and provided men, practical assistance and supply points for others. The Scottish contribution to knowledge of the Canadian Arctic was substantial. It included not only the figures whose names are commemorated in the identification of geographical features – Rae Isthmus, Richardson Island, Mackenzie River and Bay – but dozens whose pragmatic endurance of extreme privation underpinned each Arctic achievement. All of this activity strengthened the Company's hold over a huge tract of land which, with the exception of native North Americans and a few others, only its own people had the expertise to survive. And although individual endeavour was acknowledged, the conquest of the north required a spirit of collective effort which was rooted in Scottish experience.

Many of those who took part in these expeditions were either members of the First Nations or Métis, people of mixed blood, generally with either French or Scottish fathers. The Bay Company's attitude to the aboriginal population was ambivalent and inconsistent, partly cynical and partly paternalistic. The Company's commercial success depended on the active co-operation of the First Nations tribes who trapped the beaver, prepared the pelts and brought them to the trading posts. In return, they received their choice of largely practical items – knives, axes, guns, wool and flannel, kettles – all of which were cheap to produce but highly prized by the recipients. It was the company traders who valued the furs, taking into account both quantity and quality, and assessed appropriate payment. But this dependence meant that it was not in their interest to be overtly exploitative, and many saw their role as benevolent as well as commercially beneficial. As the relationship became more deeply embedded the Natives themselves grew increasingly dependent on HBC support. In a bad winter or a poor hunting season they were provided with supplies and sometimes shelter. Some were employed by the Company. Company doctors tended their sick. Unlike the Nor'Westers the HBC officially resisted the use of alcohol for trade as it undermined the ability of the Native people to hunt and deliver the goods, apart from the consumption of mostly watered-down rum having demoralising and often deadly consequences. But that official resistance was not very effective and did not last.

Native North Americans were the living proof that survival in the wilderness was possible. Without their support, many settlers would not have got through their first winter, and many of the Company's employees would never have learnt to adapt to so harsh an environment. Without the Native skills of making canoes of cedar ribs and birch bark and snowshoes of birch and sinew, of recognising the sounds and movements of animals, of reading changes in weather, of preparing and stitching hides, even of delivering babies and understanding the healing powers of plants, many Scottish communities would not have lasted. There were those aware of this debt; there were also those who resented or were repelled by the presence of an aborignal population.

Hudson's Bay Company ambivalence, or hypocrisy, is perhaps best seen in the attitude to 'country wives'. Some saw these liaisons as a convenience to be abandoned when they either returned to Scotland or married a white woman. George Simpson himself exemplifies a commonly held double standard. 'Connubial alliances are the best security we can have of the good will of the natives,' he wrote. 'I therefore recommend the Gentlemen to form connections with the principal Families immediately on their arrival...' In other words, he saw these relationships as oiling the wheels of commerce. He himself had a country wife, who was jettisoned when he married in 1830. Simpson's attitude generally to the Native population was totally pragmatic and driven by economics. He commented dryly that 'philanthropy is not the exclusive object of our visits to these Northern regions'.

Many settlers arrived fearful of the 'savages' who might appear out of the forest, and that perception lingered, on occasion fostered by actual hostile acts. The North American nations had been used by the French, the Americans and the British in the eighteenth-century wars. Their knowledge of the terrain and their wilderness skills were an asset, although their immunity to conventional military discipline caused exasperation. But their lives and traditional inter-tribal dealings were inevitably profoundly disrupted, by the fur trade and settlement as well as by European territorial quarrels. Their self-sufficiency was eroded. The most successful explorers and many HBC employees had great respect for Native skills and appreciated that their lives often depended on Native generosity and assistance. The surviving members of the Richardson and Franklin expedition of 1819, for example, were rescued from likely death by members of the Copper people who gave them venison when they were on the point of starvation.

John Rae acknowledged in some detail his debt to the Cree George Rivers, who taught him techniques of hunting, cleaning, skinning and butchering. First Nations people and Inuit accompanied him on his expeditions and he acknowledges them by name. They are individuals, not generic 'natives'. Nibitabo, like Rivers a Cree, participated in his first Arctic journey in 1846, as did two Inuit hunters and interpreters, Ouligbuck and his son William. A Dogrib guide taken on by Rae and John Richardson in 1848 proved particularly helpful:

We found our Indian companion a very great use, as he, although apparently taking us by very roundabout and crooked ways, always chose almost intuitively the best route. It was even an advantage to walk next to him, for by putting the foot exactly where he had put his, gave the surest support.

Rae was equally admiring of the skills and workmanship of Native women. Among artefacts belonging to him which are displayed in Edinburgh's Museum of Scotland is an intricately embroidered deerskin bag. Prominent among the motifs are thistles, and it is likely that these were designed by Rae himself for execution by a Cree woman. It is a striking example of a transcultural artefact.

The traditional skills Rae valued so highly were threatened by the accelerating intrusion that he and other pioneers helped to bring about. William Auld, an Edinburgh surgeon who became chief factor at Fort Churchill, wrote to the London committee of the Hudson's Bay Company concerned that all the Company's employees were complicit in the exploitation of Native peoples. He warned that wringing more 'advantages' out of 'the bloody sweat of these poor creatures' would be held against them at 'the judgement seat of Heaven'. 'There, distinctions of colour cease and it will avail but little if we transgress the rights of our coppered Indians to satiate rapacious tradesmen of a fairer hue.' But the Company believed that success depended on balancing exploitation with sustaining the vital aboriginal wilderness skills.

The erosion of traditional life and culture began from the moment of first contact between Native and incomer, and by the first decades of the nineteenth century, when increasing numbers of Scots were encountering people of the First Nations, many found little to admire. John Howison, travelling in Canada in 1819, met Tuscarora and Mohawk people, whom he believed 'incapable of improvement'. They were immune to the benefits of civilisation: 'communication with the Europeans, instead of improving them, has been the means of divesting them of those rude virtues and barbarous qualities which alone give a sort of respectability to the savage'. Howison, however, was perhaps even more critical of the white settlers he encountered in, for example, Glengarry County and the Talbot Townships. Although the Natives were 'odiously dirty', the Talbot settlers were 'offensively dirty, gross, and indolent, in all their domestic arrangements'. After an encounter with Natives, Scots and Americans occupying the same room, he concluded that the former had what he called 'negative superiority', and by virtue of being 'exalted by those virtues that generally belong to the savage... [are] more entitled to respect than either the Scotch or the Americans'.

If Howison is ambivalent, Miles MacDonell, writing a few years earlier, can find no redeeming features among the Native population. Like Howison, his view was that they were incapable of responding to 'civilising' influences: 'during their long intercourse with the whites they have not acquired one moral virtue, nor is the faintest idea of the true deity to be found among them'. Alcohol was having a devastating effect as they had little resistance to even watered spirits. MacDonell claimed that liquor was almost the only commodity for which they were willing to trade beaver pelts. They also had no resistance to the diseases the Europeans brought with them; smallpox was a particularly devastating killer.

When Adam Fergusson visited Canada in 1831 he was impressed and concerned by what he saw of Native life. He, too, described the destructive impact of Europeans, but felt that they bore a responsibility to rectify the damage:

> It is impossible not to feel a deep interest in the Aboriginals of this vast continent. As yet (comparatively speaking) nothing has been done, nor any equivalent return made, for what we have acquired from them. Probably this is not the fair criterion to assume, but unquestionably we are called

upon to make strenuous efforts towards instructing and ameliorating the condition of this race. Many a noble quality do they possess, and too many of their vices, I am afraid, must, in candour, be placed to our account.

Susanna Moodie, arriving in Canada at around the same time, recounts entirely positive relations with Natives, perhaps because the Moodies themselves treated them with respect: 'our dealings with them were conducted with the strictest integrity; and they became attached to our persons, and in no single instance ever destroyed the good opinion we entertained of them'. She clearly felt more comfortable with people of the First Nations than she did with the poor whites she encountered, specifically the Irish but also Scots, whom she found threatening. She comments on the negative effect of North America, which encouraged immigrants to have 'extravagant expectations' of equality. Respectable 'honest Scotch labourers and mechanics' descended into 'insubordination and misrule'. She was not the only middle-class emigrant to be disconcerted, even outraged, by the way respect and deference seemed to melt away when the lower classes set foot in the New World.

Robert MacDougall from Perthshire, whose Gaelic *Emigrant's Guide to North America* was published in 1841, took a great interest in aboriginal life, being particularly impressed by their child care. He found the Native people he met courteous, dignified and courageous. He was also convinced that their language was akin to Gaelic. 'They have a slow, soft, pleasant speech, merely a branch of the Gaelic language, and if those who first wrote it down had been well acquainted with Gaelic, the two languages would look remarkably similar.' This is not the only idiosyncratic opinion expressed in MacDougall's *Guide*.

John Rae worked with Métis as well as Natives, many with Scottish fathers. Their mothers were often displaced or abandoned, and the children found themselves in a kind of limbo. If their mothers returned to their tribe they were brought up as Natives, which accounts for the large number who retained both a tribal identity and a Scottish surname. Many grew up as hangers-on around trading posts and although they could be useful Hudson's Bay Company employees, their detachment from both traditional tribal life and 'polite' white society inevitably brought a legacy of problems. Some were brought up as whites. John Norquay, the son of an Orkneyman, grew up educated and well-read to become, as described by George Bryce writing in 1912, 'a man of fine disposition, and able to take his place with any class or rank of men'. He played a conciliatory role in the aftermath of the Riel Rebellion. Some Métis children went to Scotland, to be absorbed into their fathers' original communities. One who made his life in Britain was Alexander Isbister, the son of a 'half-blood' Cree and an HBC clerk from Orkney. Alexander joined the company but resigned over George Simpson's reluctance to promote Métis employees. Eventually he went to Scotland and studied law at the University of Aberdeen, and spent the remainder of his life pursuing a professional career in England.

Isbister was not only critical of the Hudson's Bay Company, on several counts. He also proved himself a champion of both Métis and Natives. He drafted a memorial to the government, published as a pamphlet, in which he wrote:

> ... we assert that they are steeped in ignorance, debased in mind, and crushed in spirit, that by the exercise of an illegal claim over the country of their forefathers, they are deprived of the natural rights and privileges of free born men, that they are virtually slaves, as absolutely as the unredeemed Negro population of the slave states of America – that by a barbarous and selfish policy, founded on a love of lucre, their affections are alienated from the British name and government, and they themselves shut out from civilisation, and debarred

from every incentive thereto – that the same heinous system is gradually effacing whole tribes from the soil on which they were born and nurtured, so that a few years hence not one man among them will be left to point out where the bones of his ancestors repose...

Isbister went on to lay responsibility for this state of affairs at the door of the Hudson's Bay Company and to request the British government to do something about it. His words have echoes in some of the literature emerging in the nineteenth century concerning the plight of Highlanders.

In terms of human relations, the challenge of the wilderness could bring out the worst as well as the best, and individual Scots were as susceptible to prejudice and blinkered perspectives as anyone else. They were quite capable of visiting on Native populations the very injustices that had driven them from Scotland. There were some who were aware, perhaps uneasily, that the displaced had become the displacers. John Galt has Bogle Corbet observe that 'this wild country' had been 'all ta'en from the Indians, who have the best right to the land, if any body has a right'. And there are examples of Scottish settlers and sojourners who developed honest and respectful relations with native North Americans. In a climate where the 'half-breed' was often presented as having the worst traits of both sides of his or her inheritance, George Bryce is unusually admiring of the Métis, whether Scottish or French in paternity. 'The half-breeds born of the union were a daring, athletic, and restless race, On the paternal side there was something of the Highlands and Islands of Scotland and of the French traders of Montreal. They were chiefly on the maternal side of the Cree nation, one of the most sturdy, brave, and persevering of the Indian peoples.' Some of British North America's most prominent Scots, for example James Douglas and Donald Smith, married Native or mixed-blood women. There were certainly those who disapproved, but it was not an impediment to social or political progress. White society in the wilderness was dominated by men. There were few white women. This author has not found any evidence of a Scottish woman linked with a native North American or Métis man.

John Buchan's novel *Sick Heart River* (1941) provides an afterword on the Scottish experience of the Canadian wilderness. It takes its Scottish hero, Edward Leithen, into the far northwest on a rescue mission when he knows that he himself does not have long to live. This is Canada a century and more after the great pioneer explorers had first endeavoured to chart the wilderness. Buchan himself had followed in their footsteps when in 1937, as governor-general of Canada, he travelled down the Mackenzie River to the Arctic. He was the first governor-general to go so far north. During his trip he camped, trekked and hunted, and met, as he recorded in an article published in the *Sunday Times*, 'the offspring of the old Hudson's Bay employees brought from Scotland and the Orkney Islands', most of whom had Scottish names. This trip was a direct inspiration for the novel, which presents the northern wilderness as an environment in which human life is both precarious and strong, diminished and uplifted. Leithen succeeds in his mission, and in the process comes to terms with the wilderness and his own death. Buchan himself died before the novel was published.

CHAPTER FIVE

A Wanderer in this New Land

*I am a wanderer in this new land which
has never been inhabited, nor has it been tilled.*
JOHN MacLEAN

WINNIPEG IS APPROXIMATELY half way between Quebec and
Vancouver. To the east stretches the Laurentian Plateau or
Canadian Shield, which covers nearly half the total area of Canada.
Its forests, muskegs, lakes, rock and tundra ensured that westward
expansion from the settlements of Upper Canada was a slow
process. West of Winnipeg, prairie stretches for hundreds of miles
to the foothills of the Rocky Mountains. Beyond the Rockies is the
Pacific coast. By 1911 Winnipeg was Canada's third largest city.
A hundred years earlier no one could have conceived that it could
thrive even as a village.

When the first Europeans arrived at the confluence of the Red
and Assiniboine rivers, south of Lake Winnipeg, the area was
inhabited by Cree and Assiniboine people. Frenchman Pierre
Gaultier de Varennes built Fort Rouge in 1735, but it didn't last.
In 1803 the North West Company established a fur trading post
on the Red River. Although hard to reach from east or west it was
more accessible from the south – the Red River rises in South
Dakota and was part of the route used by fur traders coming up
from St Paul, Minnesota. Trading posts were not seen as a focal
point of settlement. On the contrary, the fur traders themselves
were hostile to the notion of permanent populations and static
communities intruding on the wilderness on which their commerce

depended. In 1811 Alexander Mackenzie remarked: 'It has been found that colonisation is at all times unfavourable to the fur trade.' The Hudson's Bay Company resisted the encroachment of people, and as long as it controlled Rupert's Land it could be confident that its wilderness kingdom would be kept free of axes, ploughs and fences.

There were, however, homes of a sort. People, mainly men, lived at the trading posts, often for decades with little opportunity of visiting anywhere remotely like a town. For the few white women who lived at HBC factories or trading posts life was particularly hard. Letitia Hargrave, after eleven years at York Factory, accompanied her husband to Sault Ste Marie. Her pioneer life and the birth of five children had worn her to 'a perfect skeleton'. She died of cholera at the age of forty-one. At some trading posts attempts were made to raise stock and grow crops. Hudson's Bay Company factor John McLoughlin presided over Fort Vancouver which was within HBC territory until the Oregon Treaty of 1846 established the border between what would become Canada's western provinces and the US. His success at farming meant that he was able to assist the first settlers in Washington, which ran counter to HBC policy on two counts. He was supporting settlement and supporting Americans. Nevertheless, fresh vegetables, milk and meat were assets that even the most hardened wilderness men appreciated, and also helped to feed beleaguered First Nations people.

The Earl of Selkirk, with one failure and one success behind him, made a third and even more ambitious attempt at settlement. This time, inspired by reading about Mackenzie's travels, he had his sights set on land in Assiniboia, which included the Red River. He had acquired a substantial interest in the Hudson's Bay Company and was in a position to wield considerable influence, much to the dismay of the Nor'Westers. The HBC committee had become, in the words of Simon McGillivray, 'a mere machine in the hands of Lord Selkirk'. Selkirk's colonisation scheme was seen as a serious threat. McGillivray went on: 'it will require some time, and I fear cause much expense to us, as well as to himself, before he is driven to abandon the project, yet he must be driven to abandon it, for its success would strike at the very existence of the fur trade'.

Selkirk didn't abandon the project. It helped that by 1809 he owned two-fifths of the Company's shares and in 1807 had married Jane, the sister of Andrew Wedderburn Colvile who was a very influential member of the Company's governing committee. In 1811 the company granted Selkirk land for settlement, 116,000 square miles of it, equivalent to four times the area of Scotland. He paid a nominal price of ten shillings, but he had to agree to settle a thousand families within ten years. The agreement also committed Selkirk to supplying 200 men each year to work for the Company, and to allocate 200 acres each to retired HBC officers. Selkirk was to be responsible for financing the recruitment of settlers in Scotland and Ireland and getting them to Red River. It took a long time to persuade the Hudson's Bay Company to open the door to settlement. The Nor'Westers remained not at all convinced.

Selkirk despatched agents to Scotland and Ireland to recruit for the new colony, but the response was lukewarm. A small group sailed on the *Edward and Ann* from Stornoway in June 1811, but it was late September before they reached York Factory, too late in the season to continue the journey to Red River. After wintering near York Factory, a contingent of about twenty set off west but took nearly two months to reach their destination. Another small group crossed the Atlantic the following year, but the situation did not promise well for a vigorous settlement.

Selkirk had appointed Miles MacDonell as governer of the new colony. MacDonell, born in Knoydart, had fought for the British in the American Revolutionary War. His father John was one of the MacDonell brothers who had led the 1773 Knoydart emigration to New York and then to Glengarry. Selkirk was impressed by

Miles when he visited Glengarry in the course of investigating settlement possibilities, but Selkirk was not, it seems, the best judge of character. MacDonell did not provide the steady, discriminating guidance that was required, although he was determinedly upbeat in his assessment of the settlement's prospects. The initial discouraging response meant that the need to recruit was becoming urgent. Some of the 1811 and 1812 emigrants had come from Sutherland, where major upheavals were displacing and distressing the tenants of the Countess. In the spring of 1813 a further clearance was under way.

The Countess of Sutherland and her husband the Marquis of Stafford had begun a programme of clearance ten years earlier, with the twin goals, on paper at least, of making the land productive commercially and creating new communities and new occupations for her tenants. The tenants resisted. Their old way of life was being destroyed to make way for sheep runs. They were uprooted from the straths and set down in coastal villages and told to fish. Not surprisingly, for some emigration was an attractive if desperate alternative. Early in 1813 tenants of the straths of Kildonan and Clyne rebelled against their proposed displacement. William Young, the Countess's factor, appealed to her to use force. The recalcitrant Highlanders were in his view, 'banditti', savages who compared unfavourably with native North Americans. In March, troops were ordered into Kildonan. Concessions offered by the Countess calmed the situation: tenants were given more notice and were not to be forced to move until their new homes were ready for them. In spite of this, when Lord Selkirk offered to assist emigration to Red River nearly 600 people responded, although in the event many fewer actually departed.

The initial plan was to raise a regiment for service in British North America, and reward the soldiers with Red River land on which their families could immediately settle. Selkirk had not accounted for the fact that such a regiment was not actually required, and in the end he could only offer the by now customary enticements to potential settlers, the prospect of land ownership and self-determination. But as he was having to finance the project himself the numbers had to be curtailed. Later that summer ninety-four individuals assembled at Thurso in the care of young Archibald Macdonald from Glencoe. They were about to set off on what historian James Hunter has described in his book *A Dance Called America* (1994) as 'the most appalling journey ever undertaken by any of North America's many millions of European settlers'.

They crossed the Pentland Firth to Stromness, where they were to be picked up by a Hudson's Bay Company supply ship. It was the first time an emigrant group was to depart for Hudson Bay rather than the Maritimes or the St Lawrence. The *Prince of Wales* and the *Eddystone* were waiting. The ships left Stromness on 28 June, the emigrants on board the *Prince of Wales*, while travelling on the *Eddystone* were Bay Company employees. The voyage encountered one problem after another: bad weather, unusual quantities of ice in Hudson Strait, and then an outbreak of typhus. Among those who died was the surgeon who had been taken on by Selkirk to accompany the emigrants. It was late August when they reached York Factory, only to be turned away because there were not the resources to accommodate and care for them through the winter, which now loomed too close for them to move on. They disembarked instead at Fort Churchill, further north and if anything even less hospitable.

Archibald MacDonald rallied his people to build log cabins and prepare for the winter, which they could expect to be harsher by far than anything they had ever experienced. Somehow they struggled through extreme cold and savage weather, and early the following April prepared for a journey that would test their powers of endurance even further. With Hudson Bay still frozen, around forty of them were going to make the journey to York Factory overland, anxious to be in a position to head west as soon as the weather allowed. They made sledges and snowshoes, and set off, to the sound of the pipes played by Robert Gunn, on a trek of two hundred miles. In her novel *The Diviners* (1974) Margaret Laurence transforms 'Piper Gunn' into a mythic figure through the voice of Christie Logan who rehearses the tale of the Kildonan migration for the benefit of the young heroine, Morag Gunn:

> Who led the men and women and children on that march? Piper Gunn. Himself. He led them with his pipes blaring... he played the pipes like an angel right out of heaven and then like a devil right out of hell, and he kept the courage of the people beating like a drum, or like the wings of brave wild birds caught in a blizzard... I guess they must've walked through all of them frozen lands, and through the muskeg there and through the muck and mud of the melting snows, and through the hard snow itself although it was spring.

In Christie's retelling the licence of legend takes over and the 200 miles become 1,000; nevertheless, it catches both the grimness of that journey and its symbolic resonance. After two weeks of blizzards, snow blindness and exhaustion, the Kildonan migrants reached York Factory.

In late May the ice began to melt and the rivers on which the next stage of their journey depended became navigable. With such scant provisions as were available they set off once more, travelling in the heavy flat-bottomed York boats, based on a traditional Orkney vessel, which the Hudson's Bay Company used in preference to the canoes favoured by the Nor'Westers, as they were very stable and could carry three times the load. They made their way south up the Hayes River. The York boats were too cumbersome to carry like the lighter canoes, so they had to be dragged round rapids and waterfalls. When the Kildonan band finally reached the top of Lake Winnipeg they were able to sail to the lake's southern tip, and then were only a handful of relatively easy miles from their destination. To the west stretched what must have been an extraordinary sight: prairie.

There were those who did not rejoice to see this bedraggled group of families who arrived with expectations of making homes and farms where trading furs and hunting buffalo were the main activities. The North West Company and the Red River Métis both felt their way of life threatened, just as the tenants of the strath of Kildonan had felt threatened by the innovations introduced by the Countess. The Métis were, like their Cree forebears, buffalo hunters, and they knew that ploughing up the prairie would banish the beasts on which they depended. The North West Company had already conducted a campaign to denigrate Selkirk and scare potential emigrants off the whole settlement enterprise. Now that settlers, against all the odds, had arrived and taken up their 100-acre lots, the NWC encouraged hostility against them. Over the next year the Kildonan families were subject to physical harassment as well as more insidious pressures to persuade them to leave. The Métis stole their horses, trampled their crops and killed their cattle. When the Nor'Westers offered to escort them east many families were only too ready to accept.

The Sutherland emigrants had made an epic journey to reach the heart of the northern American continent. They found not only that there were others there already, but that there were other Scots. Many of the Nor'Westers were, of course, Highlanders like themselves. Many of the Métis had Highland fathers. One of the most prominent of the latter was Cuthbert Grant, son of a Cree mother and a Speyside-born officer of the North West Company, also Cuthbert Grant. Grant senior had taken NWC activities north to Great Slave Lake and was a member of Montreal's Beaver Club. His son was probably educated in Scotland – there is evidence to suggest that he spent as many as eleven years there and may have studied medicine at Edinburgh University. When his father died in 1799, young Cuthbert became the ward of William McGillivray, a partner in the North West Company, and at the age of nineteen he was taken on as an NWC clerk at Qu'Appelle River.

The lifestyle of the Red River Métis drew on the traditions of the Plains Cree. They were dependent on buffalo not only for their own subsistence but to provide pemmican, dried buffalo meat pounded with berries which was a North West Company staple. (It was the ideal wilderness convenience food, easily portable and sustaining.) They took great pride in their skills as hunters and horsemen. Cuthbert Grant was appointed by the North West Company as 'Captain of the Métis'; as such he was to prove a useful tool. Miles MacDonell assisted the campaign against the settlers by his ill-considered ban of the export of pemmican, which intensified Métis resentment. Harassment of the settlers under Grant's leadership persuaded many to give up. Only thirteen families remained. But at the north end of Lake Winnipeg the retreating band of Kildonan migrants was met by a Bay Company officer called Colin Robertson, originally from Perthshire, who persuaded them to return to Red River.

These families re-established themselves on their land, and were able to harvest their first season's crops. Another group of Sutherland emigrants arrived and the settlement began to look as if it were indeed the start of a viable farming community. The new arrivals were led by Robert Semple who replaced Miles MacDonell and constructed a fort, Fort Douglas, which perhaps made the settlers feel more secure. It was near the fort that, in the summer of 1816, this chapter of the Red River story reached a climax. When a band of Métis were seen approaching, Semple led a contingent of armed men to meet them. Whatever the intentions, shooting broke out and in the skirmish that followed Semple and nineteen of his men were killed. The episode came to be known as the Battle of Seven Oaks, named for a nearby grove of trees.

Once again, the remaining settlers retreated. They were helped by Peguis, a Salteaux chief who had already befriended them and taught them how to hunt buffalo. Meanwhile, Selkirk, now in Montreal, tried to persuade the colonial government to come to the rescue, but the settlement was the preserve of Selkirk and the Hudson's Bay Company and the government did not consider it to be their problem. Getting troops to Red River was not to be undertaken lightly. However, Selkirk himself hijacked Swiss and German soldiers who had been brought to British North America to fight in the recent war with the United States. He got them to Fort William on Lake Superior where he arrested several of the Nor'Wester nabobs who were making their annual visit, before continuing to Red River where the Métis occupying Fort Douglas were ousted. His efforts halted the complete collapse of the Red River settlement although its struggles were a long way from over. Drought, floods – the most devastating was in 1826 – and grasshopper plagues were among their adversaries, and after several decades the Métis would rebel again, although their protest this time was against the government rather than the settlers.

In 1817 Peguis along with four other chiefs of the Salteaux and Cree signed a treaty with Selkirk which in return for 100 lbs of tobacco a year gave him land for settlement along the Red and Assiniboine Rivers. Selkirk presented Peguis with a medal. Peguis himself settled with a small band on Netley Creek, a tributary of the Red, where his people farmed. He was liked and respected by the white settlers but this did not prevent them from encroaching on land that had not been agreed by the treaty.

Although some of the Sutherland families never returned to Red River, in 1821 there were over 400 people established there, over half of whom were the original settlers. That was the year the North West Company and the Hudson's Bay Company merged; the following year the Company built Fort Garry. In 1820, Selkirk, after years of ill health, disappointment and vast expenditure which he never recouped, died in France. He remains a controversial figure, much criticised for ill-planned and precipitate ventures into settlement and for his dependence on less than competent representatives. Robert MacDougall described his last attempt at settlement as 'the large, improper emigration Lord Selkirk sent to the Red River'. But he was also admired. George Bryce's description relays the view of people who knew him at Red River:

> He was tall in stature, slender in form, refined in appearance, and distinguished in manner. He had a benignant face, and his manner was easy and polite. He easily won the hearts of his colonists.

There can be little doubt that his intentions were of the best and that he genuinely wished to find a solution for dispossessed Highlanders. He expended a vast amount of time, money and effort on his settlement projects, misguided perhaps, but convinced that emigration was a beneficial move for all concerned. And ultimately there was a viable colony at Red River and the Prince Edward Island settlement thrived.

Until 1834, when governance of the Red River settlement was handed back to the Hudson's Bay Company, Selkirk's executors continued to appoint Scots as the settlement's governors. The Company followed suit, with a few exceptions. In 1828 Cuthbert Grant was appointed Warden of the Plains, thus harnessing the rebellious tendencies of the Métis. When RM Ballantyne arrived at Red River in 1843 the settlement had a population of 5,000. There were French Canadians, Scots, Natives and Métis. There were four Protestant and two Roman Catholic churches, and a courthouse at Fort Garry. The settlers were growing wheat, barley and maize and a variety of vegetables, and raising sheep, pigs, cattle and poultry. Ballantyne's fictional Jasper Derry described the settlement: 'a fine place it is, extending fifty miles or more along the river, with fine fields, and handsome houses, and churches, and missionaries and schools, and what not'. At the Bay Company trading post 'everything... a man can think of or desire' was available: 'a blanket or a file, an axe or a pair of trousers, a pound of sugar or a barrel of nails, a roll of tobacco or a tin kettle'. In 1870 the settlement acquired a new name, Winnipeg, a Cree word meaning 'muddy water' and a clue as to the sluggish nature of the river. It was still then only a village, with around fifty houses and a few stores and 'grog shops'. Ten years later it all began to change as the prospect of a transcontinental railway transformed Winnipeg from a hamlet of landlocked isolation into a focus of land boom and the gateway to a vast acreage of fertile prairie.

For half a century the Red River settlement was an anomaly. The trickle of Scottish newcomers was mainly connected with the Hudson's Bay Company, some of them arriving to take up land grants on retiring from company service. There was a gradual take up of land along the Red and Assiniboine Rivers but no incentive, and very little means, to strike out into the prairie hinterland. Red River attracted interest from the United States side of the border because it was relatively easy to reach from St Paul; American freebooters were a problem for the HBC, who struggled to control the flow of men and trade goods across the border. But in 1855 Red River struck a lone visiting American journalist as the epitome of isolation. He wrote of it:

There is a spot on this continent which travellers do not visit. Deserts, almost trackless, divide it from the habitations of men. To reach it, or once there to escape, is an exploit of which one may almost boast. It is not even marked on the maps nor mentioned in the gazetteers.

The settlement was not the start, at least not for another half century, of an expanding colony.

Emigration from Scotland continued, clearances, economic slump and potato blight all fuelling departure. It was estimated that in the summer of 1849 nearly 4,000 emigrated from Glenelg, on the west coast facing the southern end of Skye, and South Uist alone. Agents were as busy as ever. There were fifty-nine of them promoting transatlantic sailings from Aberdeen and nearby ports, and many others operating elsewhere, especially in Glasgow. In the 1840s there was a strong current of opinion in Britain as a whole that favoured emigration, both as a way of strengthening the Empire and of providing an outlet for a surplus population. In an article of July 1848 the *Illustrated London News*, which reported regularly on emigration, extolled the British people and the Empire:

> Our spirit rules the world. Our wisdom enters into the composition of the every-day life of half the globe. Our physical as well as intellectual presence is manifest in every climate under the sun. Our sailing ships and steam-vessels cover the seas and rivers. Wherever we conquer we civilise and refine... We have an insatiable energy which is of the utmost value to the world. We have spread ourselves over all regions. We have peopled North America, civilised India, taken possession of Australia, and scattered the Anglo-Saxon name and fame, language and literature, religion and laws, ideas and habits, over the fairest portions of the globe.

There is no mention of a distinctively Scottish role in all of this, and indeed many Scots struggling to clear forests and re-start their lives on Canada's frontiers may well have found it difficult to recognise themselves. The article goes on to highlight the fact that a million and a half paupers were being maintained in 'unproductive idleness' while Britain's 'magnificent colonies' were desperate for labour, which would in turn create markets for British goods: 'our colonies complain that, for want of labour, their riches remain undeveloped, and their finest territories undeveloped and untrodden'. In spite of significant numbers emigrating, a 'superabundance of population' still remained.

Whatever it was that influenced the decisions of superabundant Scots to depart it was unlikely to have been notions of having a role in colonial development. This was 1848, when rural poverty and urban deprivation were severe. Just as earlier in the century, people were leaving Scotland because they had little choice, or because they believed there were opportunities for better lives for themselves and their children. The Maritimes declined in appeal as a North American destination while Upper Canada continued to attract large numbers. In the 1840s a second wave of emigration societies, mainly in Glasgow, were setting their sights on Upper Canada. The onward journey became easier, as steamships became common on the lakes and some of the rivers and water connections were improved with the opening of canals. Some emigrants entered Canada from the United States, travelling from New York by steamship up the Hudson, then on up the Erie Canal, completed in 1825, and across Lake Ontario.

Across the prairies and on the other side of the Rocky Mountains another story was gathering momentum, independently of what was happening further east. The epic journeys of Alexander Mackenzie, Simon Fraser and others established that the Rockies were not impassable, but they did not carve out routes that could be followed by pioneer settlers. Unlike the United States, Rupert's Land did not see emigrant wagon trains crossing the prairies and the mountains in search of land. But the fur traders did it, and as with so much of Canada they opened the way for the settlement that would challenge their survival.

New Caledonia was the name given by Simon Fraser to what is now British Columbia. It was an area rich in furs, but to get them to where they could be shipped to Europe involved a transcontinental journey of spectacular difficulty. The Nor'Westers were there first, and established the initial footholds. A key figure in the next stage of fur trading in New Caledonia was a young man called James Douglas who joined the North West Company at the age of sixteen. James was the son of John Douglas, a Glasgow merchant with sugar plantations in British Guiana. James and two siblings were the product of a liaison with a Creole, possibly a Miss Ritchie. He was sent to Scotland for schooling in Lanark, before being apprenticed in 1819 to the NWC along with his brother Alexander. They sailed from Liverpool to Quebec, and then travelled on to Fort William and Ile-à-la-Crosse. Two years later the NWC was no more and James was a clerk with the Hudson's Bay Company. By the 1820s furs were being shipped from the Pacific coast to Europe via Cape Horn and the priority was to open routes for the HBC brigades bringing furs to the coast from the trading posts in the interior. James Douglas proved himself through the part he played in opening the overland route from Fort Alexandria on the upper Fraser River to Fort Okanagan and on to Fort Vancouver, a journey of around a thousand miles. For some years he was based at Fort St James, where in 1828 he and Amelia Connolly, the mixed-blood daughter of the chief factor, had a country marriage, reinforced by a Church of England ceremony nine years later. In 1830 he went to Fort Vancouver, to work under the redoubtable John McLoughlin.

Douglas was considered a rising man. He was sent on special missions, negotiating with the Russians in Alaska for example, and in 1842, when it was decided to construct a new port on Vancouver Island, it was Douglas who was selected to reconnoitre the area and supervise the building of Fort Victoria. It proved to be a significant move, as in 1846 Britain gave up any claim to the north bank of the Columbia River and conceded Oregon and Washington to the United States. For the first time, the Hudson's Bay Company had to withdraw. It lost Fort Vancouver but retained Vancouver Island, and one of Douglas's tasks was to redirect the brigade routes accordingly. The furs were now brought to Fort Langley on the lower Fraser, before being taken downriver to the coast.

Susan Moir, who in 1860 arrived in what was by then British Columbia, described in her memoirs looking out from her family's shack at Fort Hope, upriver from Fort Langley, and seeing the pack trains arrive at the HBC trading post. 'Sometimes there would be a grand stampede and the pack trains would disrupt. Horses and men could be seen through a misty cloud of dust, madly dashing all over the Hope flat, lassos flying, dogs barking, hens flying for safety anywhere.' On one occasion she was berry-picking when she encountered the leader of one of the brigades:

> I heard bells tinkling and looking up saw a light cloud of dust from which emerged a solitary horseman, the most picturesque figure I had ever seen. He rode a superb chestnut horse, satiny and well-groomed, untired and full of life in spite of the dust, heat and long journey. He himself wore a beautifully embroidered buckskin shirt with tags and fringes, buckskin pants, embroidered leggings and soft cowboy hat.

This was Angus MacDonald, born in Torridon in Wester Ross and nephew of Archibald MacDonald, who had led the 1813 Kildonan emigrants to Red River. Angus had joined the company in 1838.

Fort Victoria became the Hudson's Bay Company's New Caledonia headquarters and as part of a strategy aimed at preventing US expansion, it was decided to establish a colony on the island, a task entrusted by the government to the HBC although the Company was still resistant to making land available for settlement. Douglas was already there and seemed the obvious choice as governor of the new colony, but it was only after a false start with the inexperienced Richard Blanshard that in 1851 Douglas was appointed to the post. A continuing need was to keep a watchful eye on what the Americans were up to. Then gold was discovered on the Fraser River. It was impossible to prevent Americans from pouring in, many moving north from California, which had seen its own gold rush ten years before. It was not only Americans who were lured by these new gold fields. The fever spread all over British North America. Letitia Hargrave gives a flavour of the stories that were circulating. 'The people about the Rocky Mountains write us that gold is got in great abundance & with wonderful ease, inasmuch as a little boy dug up a thousand pounds worth with his spoon.'

Thousands came by sea, up from California, but others travelled overland. One group of around 150, many of Scottish birth or descent, travelled from St Paul to Fort Garry by steamship, then onward across the prairie in ninety-six Red River carts. The carts, famed for their squealing wooden axles, could be heard half a mile away. They crossed Athabasca, getting their first sight of the Rocky Mountains after sixty-five days. Once through the mountains at Yellowhead Pass, the party split, the smaller group making its way by the more direct but arduous land route, while the larger travelled by raft down the Fraser, northwest to Fort George before the river loops south. Several were drowned on the perilous descent.

In an effort to keep the rush for gold under control Douglas laid out townsites, built roads and generally attempted to control the explosion of activity – there were about 10,000 prospectors panning for gold on the Fraser between Forts Langley and Yale. In a report sent to the Colonial Office in June 1858, Douglas described how he was dealing with them, illustrating his fair-minded approach:

> I spoke with great plainness of speech to the white miners who were nearly all foreigners representing every nation in Europe. I refused to grant them any rights of occupation to the soil and told them distinctly that Her Majesty's Government ignored their very existence in that part of

the country, which was not yet open for the purpose of settlement, and they were permitted to remain there merely on sufferance, that no abuses would be tolerated and that the Laws would protect the rights of the Indians no less that those of the white men.

Douglas's own mixed parentage and that of his wife no doubt contributed to his respect for the Native population.

Most of what Douglas accomplished was carried out on his own initiative, with minimal government support. Four years later gold was found in the Cariboo district, further north and harder of access. To make it easier to get provisions to the mining camps Douglas initiated the construction of a major wagon road north, the Cariboo Road. Gold brought not only prospectors but a whole range of suppliers and hangers-on, and inevitably some of this surge of population remained, or was followed by those who did. People became aware that the river valleys and rolling hills were good stock-raising and fruit-growing country. In the 1850s there was growing pressure from potential settlers but the HBC resisted, anxious to keep out squatters and land speculators. Nevertheless, word was getting out that Vancouver Island and British Columbia in general had much to offer, and not only to those in search of gold.

The family of Susan Moir's father, Stratton, was from Aberdeen. She herself was born in Ceylon, where Stratton Moir had worked on a coffee plantation. After his death, Susan's mother married another Scot, Thomas Glennie, and it was with him that the family emigrated to British Columbia. Land was being made available for settlement. The journey to the Pacific coast was rather different from the route so many thousands had taken to British North America's eastern ports. They sailed from Southampton to the West Indies on a mail steamship, and journeyed by train across the Panama isthmus. Another steamship, overcrowded and much inferior to the transatlantic vessel, took them up the Pacific coast to San Francisco. After two weeks recovering from illness, the family set off again, this time to Victoria, on Vancouver Island.

Victoria was, in their eyes, not 'very much like a city', but they had letters of introduction to James Douglas, who advised them to take up a land grant on the mainland, at the head of navigation on the Fraser River. Fort Hope had been built in 1848 as one of the trading posts on the new HBC brigade route to the coast, upriver from Fort Langley. The family arrived at Hope on Susan's fifteenth birthday. It was by then 'a flourishing little town', with a church, a court house, the Hudson's Bay post, a hotel, a saloon, two stores, a butcher's shop and a blacksmith's. After a few days the family moved into a timber house 'lined and partitioned with cloth and paper'. A blanket served as an inside door, and sheets as window blinds. This middle-class family had a lot to learn. They had to do for themselves what in their previous life had been taken care of by servants. Baking bread was full of mishaps. Washing clothes was an ordeal. 'We had a tin bath we brought out with us that we used for a wash tub and as we were ignorant as to the use of wash boards, we bent over the bath and rubbed with our hands till they bled and our backs felt broken.' Beyond Hope the only 'roads' were the trails used by the HBC brigades and Natives, and any kind of travel was a major undertaking.

There was no organised emigration to British Columbia but hundreds of individual Scots made their lives there, or stayed long enough to make an imprint. By the 1860s the Hudson's Bay Company was losing its hold but its officers remained predominantly Scots. Many of the people Susan Moir encountered in her pioneering years were from Scotland, and their presence helped, psychologically as well as practically. Scots followed the gold, took up land grants, worked as surveyors and engineers, doctors and ministers. Some arrived by sea, others made the hazardous overland journey. The potential of the country gradually became known. In 1868 Susan Moir married John Fall Allison, an Englishman who had emigrated with his family to the United States and was attracted to the Fraser River by gold. Based in the Similkameen Valley on the east side of the Hope Mountains he actually made his living raising cattle and under contract to the government to open up new mountain trails. He was one of the first to see the potential for stock raising: 'There are thousands of acres of rolling hills... that are the finest kinds of grazing lands,' he commented.

Susan Moir relished pioneer life and took a lively interest in the environment and especially in the Similkameen people, recording many details of their lives and material culture in her memoirs. She took in her stride arduous mountain treks, fire and flood, winters cut off from all communication, the bearing of fourteen children, her husband's long absences on cattle drives, and the creation of a garden out of the wilderness. She was the first white woman to cross the Hope Mountains and her son was the first white baby born in the Similkameen Valley. She was helped at the birth by Suzanne, a Native neighbour. 'She thought I ought to be as strong as an Indian woman but I was not,' was Moir's comment. Perhaps not, but she was clearly tough. The rigours of pioneer life did not diminish her spirit and in spite of hardship and loss – her husband and several of her children pre-deceased her – she lived until the age of ninety-two.

In 1858 New Caledonia became the Crown Colony of British Columbia and in 1862 the Crown took back the rights over Vancouver Island and began to open up the country for colonisation; Hudson's Bay rule was coming to an end. James Douglas was now governor of the colony and faced difficulties in balancing British interests with those of the Company. The situation highlighted the increasingly anomalous situation of the Hudson's Bay Company. By 1864 Victoria had a population of around 5,000 and Vancouver Island was becoming increasingly important as a centre of mining and industry. A key figure in this development was Robert Dunsmuir, born in 1825 in Kilmarnock, the son and grandson of Ayrshire coal masters. In 1851 Dunsmuir, already married and with three children, arrived at Fort Rupert (now Port Hardy) at the north of the island, to take up employment at coal mines owned by the HBC. Many Scots were recruited to work in the mines (and also colliers from Staffordshire). The mines were not productive and the quality poor, and shortly afterwards operations were shifted to Nanaimo. Eventually the mines were taken over by the Vancouver Coal Mining and Land Company and Dunsmuir worked as a supervisor. At the same time he was conducting his own surveys, which revealed a particularly rich coal measure and enabled him to strike out on his own. On this foundation he built a hugely successful mining company. In the age of steam, coal provided the fuel for shipping, industry and railways, all of which were crucial factors in British Columbia's development.

His activities brought people and money to Vancouver Island. He employed large numbers of Chinese, who were willing to work for half the wages of whites, and was ruthless in his handling of strikes. He kept a close eye on day-to-day management, introduced the latest technology and built and operated his own fleet of colliers. He constructed Vancouver Island's railway in return for a government subsidy and a substantial land grant, with mineral rights, equal to one-fifth of the island's total area. In 1882 he stood successfully in the provincial elections, representing Nanaimo. In 1900 his son James became premier of British Columbia. Dunsmuir's success story was replicated – and excelled – by several other Scots who played key roles in the development of Canada's industry and communications. Dunsmuir's blend of shrewdness, determination and attention to detail was characteristic of the Scottish contribution.

CHAPTER SIX

The Right Sort for Canada

They are the right sort for Canada, full of grit and pluck and imbued with a spirit of independence which will make them very welcome citizens of the great Canadian Dominion.

ARGYLLSHIRE HERALD, 1906

IN THE YEAR 1820 Donald Smith was born in Forres, a small boy called John Alexander Macdonald sailed for British North America with his family, who were from Dornoch in Sutherland, and a young radical from Dundee called William Lyon Mackenzie also emigrated. In that same year at least sixty ships made the transatlantic crossing from Scottish ports, mainly from Greenock and Aberdeen, but also departing from Dumfries, Irvine, Leith, Alloa, Dundee and Montrose. They were going to ports in Nova Scotia, Cape Breton and Prince Edward Island, but above all to Quebec, sometimes continuing up the St Lawrence to Montreal. Donald Smith, John Macdonald and William Lyon Mackenzie would each play a major role on the Canadian stage.

In the 1830s most of North America north and west of the Great Lakes was unknown except to scattered groups of Native and Métis peoples, and to a few traders and travellers, mainly Scottish and French Canadian. But in Nova Scotia and Upper and Lower Canada there were areas that had been settled for more than half a century. There were communities of substance and a handful of cities, and more than a handful of cities in embryo. And where there were community and commerce, there were politics. It was inevitable that the relationship between the British government and its colonies, and between settlers and the predominant commercial interests should come to a head, and inevitable also that Scots would be involved.

William Lyon Mackenzie's parents were Highlanders from Glenshee who migrated to Dundee where his father was a weaver. By 1814, after his father's death, mother and son were running a general store and circulating library at Alyth, north of Dundee. He was twenty-five years old when he decided to leave for British North America. Although an admirer of United States democracy, he did not advocate severing the connection with Britain, and soon became impatient with the grip of Canada's Tory establishment, composed mainly of Scots. He expressed these views in pieces he wrote for the *Montreal Herald* and then, after moving to York, for the York *Observer*. In 1824 he founded his own newspaper, the *Colonial Advocate*. Through its columns he so much incensed the Tories that they retaliated by smashing his printing press.

Mackenzie was a volatile and contradictory character but he had a strong base of popular support. He was elected to the assembly of Upper Canada: the Tory-dominated assembly voted him out three times and three times his constituents re-elected him. After his first re-election, in January 1832, he and his supporters paraded through the streets of York in sleighs with bagpipes playing. Political power in Canada lay with the Tories, and most Scots in positions of influence supported them. In 1834 York was incorporated with Toronto, and Mackenzie became the city's first mayor. Three years later he published in his paper a 'Declaration of the Toronto Reformers' which spearheaded a radical protest aimed at bringing to Canada the parliamentary reforms recently won in Britain. The riots that followed caused considerable damage, although they did not develop into a full-scale rebellion. Mackenzie himself fled across the border to the United States. He eventually returned to Canada and to a somewhat tamer role in politics.

Although the protest was not successful, it brought a response in the shape of an investigation by Lord Durham, who was appointed as governor-general in 1838. The result was the Durham Report, which advocated the union of Upper and Lower Canada and a measure of self-determination without untying the colonial knot: responsible government, as it was called. It was another Scot, the Earl of Elgin, governor-general from 1847–54, who initiated a change of attitude. The British, and the Scots in particular, had been settled in permanent communities in British North America for a century. Although commercial interests were still closely tied to Britain, the people who had made their homes there – and by 1850 some had been there for several generations – were sooner or later going to forge their own political and national identity. William Lyon Mackenzie for a time saw that identity linking with the United States, which helped fuel the British government's recognition that change was necessary.

Pragmatism suggested that to maintain the colonial attachment to the mother country it would be necessary to allow the colony to grow up. The Durham Report did not provide a permanent answer; it was more a holding operation, and part of that was holding British North America against the United States. Another factor was the role of the substantial population of French Canadians, who were mainly Catholic, as were many of Scottish Highland origin. Lord Elgin's first task was to bring into being a Canadian parliament, which he did in 1848. The new government had a reforming majority and the Montreal Tories expressed their fury by pelting Lord Elgin with eggs. There were many interlinking issues involved, not least being the position of the Presbyterian church in a country with a large Scottish population where the established church was Anglican. After much argument a Canadian Presbyterian church emerged on an equal footing with the Anglicans, Catholics and Methodists, but it was Scottish enough to keep alive the divisions that characterised Presbyterianism in Scotland. As in Scotland, in 1843 there was a split that created a Free Church in Canada, and by 1861 the latter had 50 per cent more members than the Kirk. Scottish Calvinism remained a strong current in Canadian life.

Scottish Presbyterian suspicion of Catholicism also affected political and religious life. Lower Canada (Quebec) remained largely French and largely Catholic, although there were significant Scottish communities. In the 1830s the French-Canadians, led by Louis-Joseph Papineau, were agitating for more separation from Britain and against a united Canada. This came to a head in 1837 with an open rebellion, a little before Mackenzie's protest, which was put down by British troops. When after 1837 the issue of reparations emerged there were those who opposed the inclusion of French Canada. There were also some who objected to the inclusion of Catholics in the co-established churches. This was more than a religious issue. Each of the four churches received a share of the clergy reserves, money made available by the sale of land originally allocated for church use. The division between the French- and English-speaking populations of Canada was complicated by the fact that many of the Highland Scots communities were Catholic – and Gaelic-speaking. The first Catholic archbishop of Upper Canada was Alexander MacDonell from Glengarry and Scots were prominent in all aspects of the church. The first Anglican bishop of Upper Canada was John Strachan from Aberdeen.

The debate about Canada's political and religious future continued, and Scottish voices were prominent. One of the loudest was that of George Brown, editor of the Toronto *Globe*. In 1837 at the age of nineteen George Brown had emigrated with his family to New York, where his father, a radical town councillor from Edinburgh, had started a newspaper for Scots in North America. George himself was born in Alloa, a small port on the Firth of Forth, where his father for a time helped to run the Alloa glassworks. Six years after arriving in New York the family moved to Toronto and founded the *Globe*, which became the mouthpiece of support for responsible government and also an expanded Canada. Brown wanted self-government without separation, and a 'British America' that stretched from 'Labrador to Vancouver Island and from our own Niagara to the shores of Hudson Bay'. In 1852 he was elected to parliament. Over the years his views modified and he became a supporter of the idea of confederation, the coming together of the British North American provinces to form an independent national entity. He was a key player in the 1864 convention that laid the foundations for confederation, which followed three years later. Throughout his political life, Brown continued his editorship of the *Globe*, which started as a weekly but by 1853 was a daily paper with probably the largest circulation in British North America. But in a sense it was the *Globe* that killed him. He was shot in a confrontation with an inebriated employee whom he had sacked. Although it was only a flesh wound, he died some time later of blood poisoning.

In 1874 a young man called John Clay, from near Kelso in the Scottish Borders, met George Brown, who by this time was running a farm near Brantford, Ontario. In the 1850s Brown had acquired land in Lambton County which he sold off as farm and town lots, creating the village of Bothwell. He built roads and mills, and dealt in lumber. When oil fields were discovered on his land, he sold up to an oil syndicate but retained his involvement in agriculture. Clay himself came from a farming background, and was interested in what Brown was doing to improve livestock in Ontario. Clay described Brown: 'He was a marvellous man, sanguine, patriotic, indomitable, far-seeing politically, adored by his followers, hated by his opponents.' Two years later Brown returned to Scotland on a visit to set up a company that would ship out good breeding stock of cattle, horses, sheep and pigs. He persuaded the Edinburgh publishers Thomas and William Nelson to get involved, and married their sister Anne. Clay himself was taken on to purchase Clydesdale horses and arrange the shipping out of stock. The venture was not a success, and Clay made another visit to Ontario to try to sort it out.

Many Scots came to North America hoping for both physical space – land, and social space – freedom from the constraints of class and lack of franchise. John Clay is a good example of a man who chose to leave Scotland. He was not forced to leave his home and economic necessity was not driving him. But he did feel that opportunities in Scotland did not measure up to his ambitions and abilities. In his memoirs he criticised the 'social segregation of classes' and went on to list other factors that explained his departure: 'a smothering of ambition, a fierce fight against political independence, the neglect of ability, the silent, sarcastic repression of any forward movement, the absence of a generous uplift, the extravagance of our landed proprietors and their utter inability to meet adverse times'. Clay went on from Canada to have a successful, if not altogether untrammelled, career as a rancher in Wyoming.

The issue of the now united Canada and its relationship to the other British North American provinces became a prominent feature of political debate. There was a growing movement for confederation, the bringing together of all the provinces under a single legislature. One of the leading voices in this campaign was that of George Brown. Another was that of John Alexander Macdonald, who had settled with his family in Ontario and entered politics in 1843 as a member of the Conservative Party. He became prime minister in 1857, and ten years later formed the new dominion's first government. The Dominion of Canada was born as a result of the British North American Act passed in 1867. Initially the members of the confederation were Quebec and Ontario (previously Canada), New Brunswick and Nova Scotia. Other provinces followed: Manitoba in 1870, British Columbia the following year, Prince Edward Island in 1873, and Alberta and Saskatchewan in 1905.

The framework of governance had changed, but this did nothing to weaken the close links between Scotland and Canada.

Many of those prominent in government were Scots or of Scottish descent. Alexander Galt, for example, the son of John Galt, was another Scot who helped to take British North America down the road to confederation. He was finance minister in John A Macdonald's Conservative government, and in 1880 became Canada's first high commissioner in London. In any single page of Canada's political history in the nineteenth century Scottish names are likely to appear, as establishment Tories and members of the Family Compact (the name given to the Scottish Tory network), as radicals and reformers, as mavericks, as representatives of the British government. The first Liberal prime minister of Canada was Alexander Mackenzie, a stonemason born in Perthshire who had emigrated to Sarnia, Ontario in 1842. The vigorous Scottish presence in Canadian politics was a powerful influence in the way the Canadian nation took shape. It may have something to do with the fact that in Scotland itself at this time there was little scope for political activity.

The Dominion of Canada's first government, led by Macdonald, had responsibility for a vast, strung-out patchwork of provinces massively divided by distance, wilderness and mountains, and only partially connected by rivers and lakes. The Durham Report had commented on the lack of roads and communications in Upper Canada, where settlement was growing and communities taking root. Beyond Red River, in Manitoba, which joined the Dominion in 1870, there was virtually no settlement. In British Columbia the discovery of gold had forced the pace of development but it was still not much more than a scattering of infant communities connected, if at all, by dangerous waterways and rough mountain trails. Manitoba was a long way from Toronto. British Columbia was a great deal further, with a daunting mountain barrier adding to the distance. Before British Columbia joined the confederation it made a condition. A railway link would have to be built across the continent. The construction of a transcontinental railway dominated the political landscape for the next fifteen years.

And the railway was itself dominated by Scots. The United States had completed its first transcontinental railroad in 1869. Crossing Canada was even more challenging, and it took years of argument over the idea and fierce contention over the route before it began to look like a reality. Canada's first railways had begun to be developed in the 1830s and were making a huge difference to the speed and experience of travel. But at every stage routes were the subject of dispute, as communities and business interests put their competing arguments for their particular railway needs. There were political factors as well.

There was a strong Scottish engineering tradition and it is no surprise to find Scottish names among those who surveyed and engineered Canada's railways. One of those who contributed most was Sandford Fleming, born in Kirkcaldy, Fife, in 1827. Encouraged by a cousin to try their luck in Canada, in 1845 Sandford Fleming and his brother David left Glasgow for Quebec on the *Brilliant* and then made their way upriver to Montreal on a paddle steamer making her maiden voyage. It turned out to be a memorable trip. The steamer was too wide for the river locks, and the paddle boxes had to be removed to allow her through. This deprived her of power, so the vessel had to be hauled upriver. The brothers continued their journey by river barge up the Ottawa to Bytown, then a lumber town but later to become Ottawa, the dominion's capital, on to Kingston on Lake Ontario, and then on the corduroy (log) road to Peterborough, where their cousin Dr John Hutchison lived. The journey from Kirkcaldy to Peterborough took ten weeks.

Fleming gradually established himself as a surveyor in Toronto, where he was the first to map the harbour, and in 1852 was taken on by the Ontario, Simcoe and Huron Railway as assistant engineer. The railway opened the following year. He continued as a railway engineer, leading the survey of the Intercolonial Railway in the 1860s, until in 1871 the government authorised the survey of a transcontinental line. Sandford Fleming was appointed chief engineer and took on as his secretary George Grant, a Presbyterian minister from Halifax whose father came from Banffshire. He was a tough character, possibly hardened by his experience of losing a hand in an agricultural accident, who would go on to become an academic and educator.

They were undertaking to survey a territory that included vast tracts that were little known and formidably resistant to a human presence. There had been expeditions in 1857 and 1858 looking for routes to the Pacific, but their reports were conflicting. The official British expedition, led by Irishman John Palliser, was a two-year exploration of the terrain west from Lake Superior to the coast. With him was James Hector, an Edinburgh geologist, who negotiated a pass through the Rockies which eventually became the route of the Canadian Pacific Railway. While making his way through his horse stumbled, unseated and kicked him. The unconscious Hector narrowly escaped being buried alive by his companions, who were convinced he was dead. The incident gave the name Kicking Horse to the pass. James Hector went on to have a distinguished career in New Zealand, appointed government geologist in 1861 and becoming director of Wellington's colonial museum and botanical gardens.

Fleming's survey was to be carried out in four sections: from the Ottawa valley to Nipigon on Lake Superior; from Nipigon to Fort Garry, Red River; from Fort Garry to the Rocky Mountains, and from the Rockies to the Pacific coast. The survey took 800 men into the field and involved looking for a way through the most extreme terrain imaginable: solid rock and solid forest, morasses of swamp of unknown depth, prairie cut by erratic coulees, formidable mountains, ferocious rivers. The surveyors worked through the savage cold of winter and intense heat of summer, and endured mosquitoes and blackflies, flash floods, avalanches, and forest and prairie fires. The biggest challenges were carving a way through the rock and over muskegs north of Lake Superior and finding a route through the mountain barrier and on to the coast. In 1872 Fleming and Grant themselves made one continuous journey across the Great Lakes, through the unforgiving rock and muskeg of the Laurentian Plateau to Winnipeg, and then on across the prairie by way of the North Saskatchewan River and Fort Edmonton to the Yellowhead Pass, which Fleming recommended as the best route through the Rockies. From the Yellowhead they struck southwest, down through Kamloops to Burrard Inlet. They travelled over 5,000 miles in 103 days.

The financial and political interests involved in building a transcontinental railway were labyrinthine, and undoubtedly added to the cost of what was always going to be a vastly expensive enterprise. There was a great deal at stake for a great many people. Routes were argued over and changed several times. Accusations and counter-accusations, concerning malpractice and underhand methods, flew back and forth. Fleming was one of many caught up in these: he was accused of being careless and unbusinesslike with funds. Macdonald's government, which supported the railway, in 1873 lost an election to Mackenzie's Liberals, who declared the transcontinental project madness. Even so, the Canadian Pacific Railway Act was passed in 1874 and stretches of line began to be built on a piecemeal basis. The whole gargantuan enterprise not only needed political will and practical expertise, it needed a very large amount of money. It was 1880, with Macdonald back in power, before six men got together to form the syndicate which created the Canadian Pacific Railway Company: Richard Bladworth Angus, a Scot, was general manager of the Bank of Montreal; James J Hill, Canadian-born of Scottish parents, had already proved his mettle building railroads in the United States; JS Kennedy was a New York banker, also of Scottish origins; Duncan McIntyre controlled the Canadian Central Railway; Sir Stafford Northcote was governor of the Hudson's Bay Company; and George Stephen, son of a Banffshire carpenter. Stephen, who grew up in Craigellachie on the River Spey, left Scotland in 1850 at the age of twenty-one to work in a relative's Montreal textile business. For $25 million and 25 million acres the syndicate took on the construction of nearly 2,000 miles of track and the operation of the railway that would run on it.

Backing the syndicate was Donald Smith, a cousin of George Stephen. He, Stephen and Hill had two years previously bought up the failing St Paul and Pacific Railway, and completed its connection to Winnipeg. Smith was from Forres, not far from Stephen's Dufftown birthplace. He had come to Canada in 1838 to join the Hudson's Bay Company, his way smoothed by a letter of introduction to George Simpson from his uncle John Stuart, an HBC chief factor. Smith spent thirty years in Labrador, where he laboured for the Company in extraordinary isolation (although he met and married his wife there) and slowly made his way up the ladder. After twenty-four years he became chief factor and his progress accelerated. In another four he was head of the Montreal department and in 1883 he became a director and major shareholder of the company. His change in fortune was partly the result of the way he dealt with the Métis rebellion of 1869, led by Louis Riel.

In 1867 the Hudson's Bay Company had agreed to relinquish its prairie territory, surrendering its monopoly of land rights. The Métis holding land in the Red River area felt threatened by the prospect of the HBC making way for an influx of settlers, who would inevitably have an impact on their traditional way of life. This prompted them to rebel. A young man of twenty-five called Louis Riel emerged as their leader. By the end of 1869 they had taken over the Red River settlement and were holding prisoners. Donald Smith was identified as the man to deal with this difficult situation and was duly despatched to Red River to negotiate. Troops followed, and Riel was eventually sent into exile in the United States. The incident made

Macdonald realise, if he had not before, that good communications were going to be vital to shaping a cohesive nation.

It was Donald Smith's first trip west and it made him aware both of the isolation of Red River and the potential for creating a link that would open up the prairies. A railway would bring people, create markets and move goods and products to service those markets, as well as ensuring the speedy movement of troops, a concern of the prime minister. On the doorstep of Winnipeg there was already the St Paul and Pacific Railroad. It was bankrupt, but with a fresh injection of cash it had the potential to complete a link which would be a gateway to the outside world, albeit an American, not a Canadian gateway. Donald Smith and his cousin George Stephen seized the opportunity.

George Stephen's inheritance of his relative's textile firm led to him becoming a respected member of Montreal's business community. He became a director of the Bank of Montreal and, in 1876, its president. He had risen faster than his cousin Donald and had a reputation as an unobtrusive but astute operator. They clearly made a formidable duo. The completion of the St Paul and Pacific was the prelude to the big project. Prime minister Macdonald was committed to a transcontinental rail connection, which he saw as crucial to meld the young dominion into 'a homogenous whole', as he put it in his 'Last Address to the People of Canada'. Looking back at what he evoked as a period of heroic endeavour, he went on:

> Undeterred by the pessimistic views of our opponents – nay, in spite of their strenuous, and even malignant opposition, we pushed forward that great enterprise through the wilds north of Lake Superior, across the western prairies, over the Rocky Mountains to the shores of the Pacific, with such inflexible resolution, that, in seven years after the assumption of office by the present Administration, the dream of our public men was an accomplished fact...

Voiced by the 'malignant opposition' was the belief that the project was lunatic and doomed to failure; there was also outrage at the cost. Macdonald persuaded his government to provide millions of dollars in subsidy. The laying of track over what some felt to be impossible terrain proved much more difficult and much more costly than anticipated, and the Canadian Pacific Railway Company repeatedly had to ask the government and the banks for more. The company's directors drew also on their personal resources. There were several moments when progress faltered so drastically it looked as if the track could go no further. Strikes were threatened. Stephen, whose main role was to keep the money flowing in, was more than once ready to give up. The army of men – surveyors, engineers, suppliers of material, locomotive drivers and firemen, navvies – had to be supported by a second army which ensured they were sheltered and fed, their tools supplied and maintained, their belongings transported when the construction camps moved on. These armies included many Scots, as well as Irish, English, French, recent immigrants from Europe, people of the First Nations, and Métis. In British Columbia large numbers of Chinese were taken on as navvies; they worked for much less than anyone else and accepted appalling conditions without complaint. The steely resolve of the moguls who drove the project depended on a diverse and volatile collection of individuals who endured relentless hardship for little reward.

With the 3,000 miles of railroad from Halifax to Port Moody nearly completed, Louis Riel emerged again at the head of the disaffected Métis. It was 1885, and the CPR was floundering yet again, with the government refusing to throw yet more money into its seemingly insatiable maw. The second Riel Rebellion was a godsend to the beleaguered syndicate, who had by this time put a great deal of their own money into the railway. Nothing could have more dramatically highlighted the problems of the governance of territory without communication links. The government now acknowledged that the railway was a prerequisite for the taming of the wilderness and its people, and voted more money for the CPR. The Canadian Pacific Railway was completed in November 1885, taking not Fleming's recommended route through Yellowhead Pass but James Hector's route further south which crossed the continental divide at Kicking Horse Pass and involved a perilous and stomach-churning descent on the western side. The last spike was driven in by Donald Smith at a little place in the Selkirk Mountains called Craigellachie, the same name as the village of George Stephen's upbringing. The hammering of the spike was followed by silence, then a resounding cheer and the whistles of the locomotives. Riel was captured, tried, and hanged a week after the ceremony. Two years later the line was extended from Port Moody to Vancouver. This triggered an industrial boom, with foundries, sawmills and fish canneries attracting money and labour.

Donald Smith, Sandford Fleming was to write later, was 'more than the representative of the railway company, his presence recalled the memories of the Mackenzies, Frasers, Finlaysons, McLeods, MacGillivrays, Stuarts, McTavishes and McLoughlins who in past generations penetrated the surrounding mountains'. Fleming himself, who had already designed Canada's first postage stamp and founded the Canadian Institute, equally made his mark by devising a system of Standard Time, which brought order to the chaos of time changes highlighted by speedier travel. Having played his part in the railway reaching the Pacific, he continued to look west with plans for a Pacific cable. He was appointed chancellor of Queen's University in Kingston. It was not the end of the road, either, for Donald Smith and George Stephen. Their business careers continued, and Smith added politics to his activities. He built a home near Winnipeg and was elected to the Manitoba provincial assembly. In 1889 he became governor of the Hudson's Bay Company. In 1896 he was knighted, the same year that he was appointed Canada's high commissioner in London, and the following year he was made a baronet, becoming Lord Strathcona. George Stephen became Baron Mount Stephen in 1891. Stephen spent his last years in England. Smith maintained his Scottish connections, purchasing an estate in Glencoe and then, in 1900, the island of Colonsay. Both men lived into their nineties.

George Stephen, a quieter, less flamboyant man than Smith, beavered away out of the public eye. Smith had extraordinary energy, perhaps fuelled by his thirty-year exile in the Labrador wilderness. Although nine years Smith's junior, Stephen was running his own business and was a director of the Bank of Montreal when Smith's career had hardly started. But Smith made up for lost time. The London *Daily News* commented, 'You talk with him, and it is as if Canada stands before you, telling her astonishing story.' He became simultaneously an icon of Canada, of the British Empire and of Scotland, and the fact that he was ruthless and not exactly straightforward in his financial dealings certainly contributed to his success and possibly to his image. 'With no advantages of birth or fortune, he made himself one of the great outstanding figures of the Empire,' said his obituary in *The Times*. Stephen, in his more reticent way, was no less an emblem of all three. Canada's 'astonishing story' was a narrative in which leading roles were taken by Scots, many of whom achieved what they did by sailing close to the wind of probity.

In 1869 the infant dominion consisted of four provinces and three cities. Montreal had a population of 100,000; Quebec and Toronto 60,000 each. Its neighbours were the United States, shaken by its recent civil war but nevertheless increasingly self-confident, and the domain of the Hudson's Bay Company, weaker now, but still formidable. The process of absorbing HBC territory began, and having begun, it was important for the new dominion's credibility to settle it. Manitoba was the first candidate and the Dominion Lands Act of 1872 was intended to bring people to the prairies. Townships were divided into 640-acre sections, to allow for farms large enough for commercial wheat production. Settlers could take up a quarter section on payment of a ten dollar registration fee, and once they could demonstrate three years of occupation and cultivation of the land they could file a claim of ownership. Later amendments allowed for a sponsor to support emigrants committed to settling in the prairies to the tune of a 500 dollar loan. But the prairies in the 1870s were not an attractive proposition. Getting there was a challenge, and once there farmers found they were contending with what seemed to be an endless cycle of difficulty.

Pioneering in the prairies was as daunting as it had been in the backwoods a hundred years earlier, although it was sod houses that were the first homes, not log houses. The land was richly fertile, but ploughing, planting and harvesting still involved relentless labour, and neither the productive soil nor hard work made a difference when drought, or floods, or grasshoppers struck. Even with the prospect of the railway, it was hard to persuade settlers to make the journey beyond the Great Lakes. But there began a trickle of the discouraged and disaffected from communities in Nova Scotia, Ontario and the Eastern Townships, whose decades of battling against forest and rocky terrain had brought little reward. For some, the reality of Manitoba was not encouraging. 'I am now a wanderer in this new land,' wrote John MacLean in his native Gaelic, 'which has never been inhabited, nor has it been tilled,' and he went on to lament the absence of the 'relatives and compatriots' he had left behind in Ontario.

The Canadian government renewed its efforts to bring people to Canada, especially to the west. Agents, including CPR agents promoting settlement of railway land, travelled through Scotland giving illustrated lectures and handing out promotional leaflets, spelling out the availability of assisted passage and railway land grants. In the early 1880s Winnipeg, with the transcontinental rail connection beginning to become a reality, experienced a land boom and within ten years its population leapt to nearly 40,000. (By 1904 its railway yards were the biggest in the world.) But enticing people into virgin territory was another matter. Some unfortunates were persuaded by the promise of a branch line link which didn't materialise, or came many years later.

As the Canadian Pacific Railway was forging its way west, in the Scottish Highlands and Islands there was another phase of protest against high rents and landlord oppression. The Crofters' War of the 1880s drew attention to the predicament of tenants paying rents they could not afford for insufficient land to support their families. Landlords were again making efforts to shift the people whom they regarded as surplus to requirements, or who might cause trouble. Lady Emily Gordon Cathcart, the daughter of John Gordon of Cluny, whose clearance in 1850 of South Uist and Benbecula had been particularly uncompromising, responded to the crofters' need for land by removing the crofters. She arranged for ten families to leave in the spring of 1883, paying their passage to what became Saskatchewan. The following year 200 more people joined them, settling around Wapella and Moosomin. The response of the vanguard families was at first positive. The summer was unusually fine and, as they had arrived in May, they were able to get their first crops in the ground in good time. 'I am very glad for my change from the old Benbecula to the new Benbecula,' said Angus MacCormic in a report to the Napier Commission. Norman McDonald remembered that the potatoes planted in early June produced a good crop, although the family's sod shack burnt down.

The 1884 emigrants were not so impressed. Drought blighted their efforts to establish productive farms and they were soon cursing their exile, and Lady Emily's part in it. But the initial reaction encouraged the authorities to see emigration as part of the solution to the 'problem' of the Highlands and Islands; and of course, this suited the landlords, even when they themselves contributed financially. The Land League, on the other hand, saw emigration as a means of side-stepping the need for radical reform.

A particularly strong advocate for emigration was Malcolm McNeill, a Poor Law Inspector and Secretary to the Napier Commission. On his recommendation it was decided in the spring of 1888 to go ahead with an organised emigration from Lewis to the northwest of Canada. He went to Lewis to recruit emigrants. The British government provided £11,000 to fund passage and loans to enable families to get established, on condition that £2,000 was raised by public subscription. The Canadian government also agreed to support the scheme. Lady Matheson, the proprietor (widow of James Matheson), believed Lewis to be over-populated and was more than happy to co-operate. Her uncompromising view was that the land was hers to use as she wished, regardless of the welfare of her tenants.

Arrangements were made with precipitate haste. McNeill was hoping to recruit young wage-earners rather than families, but in the event included twenty-one families in the total. They had less than a week to prepare for departure. They had to sort out their affairs and sell those belongings they could not take with them. To pay off debts, some of which were considerable, might mean spending the loans intended for settlement in Canada. It all happened with such speed, that when they disembarked at Quebec they did not know where they were going: there had not been sufficient discussion with the Canadians, and no land had yet been allocated. They were met and looked after by a CPR official and members of the local St Andrews Society. Meanwhile a second group, ninety-seven individuals recruited from Harris, sailed from the Clyde in early June. McNeill was back in Lewis in September to get a third group together. He was instructed to select families who would not be a financial burden on the government; in fact, he chose the poorest. Landlords saw emigration as a means of expelling paupers and trouble-makers. The following spring, another group followed.

Although the Canadian authorities were keen to encourage settlement, they were not prepared for this rush of emigrants with minimal financial resources. The first group was sent west and arrived in the township of Killarney, west of Winnipeg and near the US border. The settlers had understood that they would be helped by the Canadian government to get started, but no cash was made available, and no seed for planting. Local shopkeepers were persuaded to give them credit. One of them, TJ Lawlor, was highly critical: 'Fancy a people taken away from fishing scenes and dumped upon the prairies – and no provision made for seed. Gaelic may be a very nice and expressive dialect but you cannot raise wheat from it, and these people had nothing else.' If anything, the shock of the prairies was greater than the shock of the forested wilderness experienced by the Nova Scotia pioneers a century earlier.

The Killarney settlers had a discouraging initiation and several years of struggle and debt in front of them. The group that left Lewis in 1889 had an even harder time. They were sent to Saltcoats, further west in what was still Assiniboia (it became the province of Saskatchewan in 1905). One of the emigrants, Norman McDonald, recalled his journey as a child by steamer to Glasgow and then on the Allan Line's *Scandinavian* to Halifax. From Halifax they travelled by train to Saltcoats, where they were housed in an 'Immigrant Shed' and railway boxcars because of delays in allocating land and getting houses built. In a response to a Saskatchewan Archives questionnaire he remembered:

> My chief impression of the early years was the great loneliness of prairie life, after living in the Islands where people were crowded together. We went to Saltcoats about once a week, a day's journey by oxen. After the first church was built in the district in 1896, we went to church every Sunday. All travel was by ox wagon or on foot, as none of the settlers had horses in the early years.

By the time the Saltcoats settlers had somewhere to go it was too late in the season for planting, and so there was no crop. It was difficult to get employment locally, and shopkeepers, unlike those in Killarney, were reluctant to give credit. The settlers felt they had no option but to appeal to the Scottish Office for support. Poor harvests in the early 1890s compounded their problems. Over half the families who settled in the Saltcoats area abandoned their farms.

Although the Killarney and Saltcoats settlers had clearly been hustled into a poorly thought-out scheme, there were those who were highly critical of the settlers themselves. Lord Lothian, Scottish Secretary at the time, had urged state support for emigration and did not listen when the Canadian High Commission tried to slow things down; he believed that the scheme was good but the settlers themselves were not up to the mark. Many of those in Canada who witnessed their struggles saw them as unwilling as well as ill-equipped pioneers. In 1890 Lady Aberdeen visited the Killarney settlement. Although her publicly-expressed impressions were upbeat, privately she wrote of the 'inexpressible dreariness of these everlasting prairies, with their serpentine black trails winding through them'. Families with half a dozen or a dozen children were living in wooden shacks, their energies entirely taken up with 'the struggle to live'. Many years later Hugh MacLennan captured the loneliness and emptiness of the prairie:

> I remember the feeling of fear it gave me as a boy when my mother told me of a relative who had gone to Saskatchewan from Nova Scotia, and how she had watched her son walking alone across the prairies to school until he became a dot on the horizon.

By the early twentieth century hundreds of thousands had flooded into the prairie provinces from all over Europe, and yet it was still possible for an individual barely to register on the vast landscape. Scots communities were distinctive but not so prominent as they were further east, and other groups were making a significant impact. The first to make a success of prairie farming were Mennonites from the Ukraine. The Ukrainian community features in the series of novels by Margaret Laurence set in and around the fictional town of Manawaka, based on Neepawa west of Winnipeg where she grew up. In *A Jest of God* (1966) she characterises the Scots and the Ukrainians in the voice of her heroine Rachel Cameron:

> Half the town is of Scots descent and the other half is Ukrainian. Oil, as they say, and water. Both came for the same reasons, because they had nothing where they were before. That was a long way away and a long time ago. The Ukrainians knew how to be better grain farmers, but the Scots knew how to be almightier than anyone but God.

But it was grain rather than God that made Manitoba and the prairie provinces viable. In the 1870s Manitoba was producing more wheat than furs. The character of farming was changing. On his Red River farm William Dalrymple was planting nearly 30,000 acres with wheat. He harvested 1,000 acres a day, using seventy-five reaping and binding machines and 450 labourers. W Fraser Rae, who visited Manitoba around 1880, commented on Manitoba farming practice: 'the whole arrangements are designed to assimilate the production of grain to the operations of a manufactory... the farmer is a capitalist; the farm-labourer is called a "hand" and treated as one.' Further west in Alberta cattle ranching was developing, although its 1880s heyday was brief. By the end of the century grain production had taken over.

The kingdom of the Hudson's Bay Company was coming to an end. Politics and communications were now the realms of Scottish adventuring. This new Scottish territory is captured in the novels of Frederick Niven, writing in the 1930s and '40s. *The Flying Years* (1935) takes the hero Angus Munro from Highland eviction to Red River, where family friends are already established, speaking Gaelic and playing the pipes in a kitchen 'like an old Scots interior'. After the death of his parents Angus goes west, a journey which he repeats when he returns to Red River after spending some years back in Scotland. The narrative encompasses prospecting for gold, relations with Native peoples and Métis, farming, the coming of the railway, and Angus Munro's eventual employment as an Indian agent in Saskatchewan. It chronicles the process of transition from Scot to Scottish Canadian. *The Transplanted* (1944) in a sense takes up the same story with a different cast of characters, bringing it into the twentieth century. Robert Wallace is a civil engineer from middle-class Glasgow, surveying for railway and mining companies, and consciously evoking the pioneering spirit of earlier generations. His compatriot Jock Galbraith is also from Glasgow, but from the impoverished Gorbals. Jock has wandered extensively in the Canadian and American west: 'everywhere I went was better than the Gorbals,' is his conclusion. Robert is more ambivalent. As he leaves Scotland for the second time, after a visit to his family in Glasgow, that ambivalence is highlighted: 'He was the unwilling exile looking back on a receding shore. He was the willing exile looking beyond the sea to the country that had adopted him, that he had adopted.'

Angus Munro and Robert Wallace are both pioneers, typical in different ways of the Scottish imprint on Canada generally, and Canada's frontiers, geographical and commercial, in particular. 'What a part you have played in the making of this west,' says Jock Galbraith to Robert Wallace, and goes on to list his achievements:

> You opened up the valley... you bought land with an eye to the future and sold it again to farmers; you brought in the

railway... And there would have been no Elkhorn but for you. When the settlers began to complain they hadna enough markets, who started the Creamery and boosted Elkhorn butter? Who was responsible for the erection of the smelter, the power plant, for all that made this district what it is?

Niven's fiction gives us a heroic version of the Scottish pioneer, but there were plenty of real-life examples to provide his inspiration. Angus and Robert, though operating on a large canvas, are small-scale pioneers in comparison with George Simpson or Donald Smith, but any attempt to translate the latter pair into fiction would have stretched credibility. They were legends in themselves.

Canada is a country where there will always be frontiers, thanks to the challenge of its geography and its extremes of climate. But in settlement terms, the prairies, and the valleys on the far side of the Rockies, were seen as the last territory of community building. Many of the Scots who settled there had moved west from Nova Scotia or Ontario, some to start again as farmers, others to find employment in industry or mining. But there was, especially between the world wars when the Depression revived all the old anxieties about a redundant population, still a flow of Scots from the old country. The last chapter in terms of organised emigration to the prairie provinces unfolded in the 1920s, with the people who in April 1924 left the Hebrides on the *Marloch*, in a venture organised by Father Andrew MacDonell. They were bound for Red Deer in northern Alberta, where they established the community of Clandonald. They did not thrive. After five years, poor crops and lack of employment possibilities meant that many of the families were in a bad way. They had to be helped with cash, seed and second-hand clothing. There was little prospect of their repaying the loans they had received to get them started. Forging a new life in Canada was no easier for them in the twentieth century than it had been for Scottish settlers in the eighteenth.

The two world wars brought Scottish Canadians to Scotland as members of the forces, and led to some rediscovering the origins of their forebears. After World War II there were continued inducements to emigrate, and Canada was seen as an attractive proposition for Scots seeking opportunities that post-war Scotland did not offer. Many left Scotland and thrived; others found that, for a variety of reasons, Canada did not suit them, and so they returned.

If steam in the mid-nineteenth century brought the New World closer, in the mid-twentieth another transport revolution brought it closer still. Air travel means that those who leave Scotland now know that it is unlikely to be forever, and that it is easy to stay in touch with those they leave behind. Thousands of Scots who have no intention of emigrating are familiar with Canada because they have friends and relatives there, from Cape Breton to Vancouver Island.

CHAPTER SEVEN

True Canadians

His bairns ir true Canadians
Dey wear da kilt an proudly shaa wis foo ta dö
da sword dance...
CHRISTINE DE LUCA

OVER THE WINTER of 1835–36 John Richardson was at Fort Franklin on Great Bear Lake with about fifty men, women and children. They were taking part in John Franklin's second expedition. Most were Scots, but there were also Natives and Métis in the group. They had built log cabins to shelter them through the severe far northern winter, and game was plentiful. Among this little community were a piper and a fiddler. In a letter home Richardson wrote of 'that romantic attachment which a Scotchman, in his wanderings, feels towards the land of his birth'. On the day after Christmas and again at New Year they celebrated with music and dancing. Similar scenes recur in many accounts of Canada's pioneering past. Wherever there were Scots, it seems, there was music.

The pipe band of Simon Fraser University near Vancouver is one of the best in the world and frequently outplays Scottish bands. There are pipe bands all over Canada, along with piping and Highland dancing societies. It is often said that Scottish Canadians cherish the culture of the Gael more enthusiastically than do the Scots in Scotland. Although the number of Gaelic speakers in Canada is dwindling, as it is in Scotland, traditional Scottish music is vigorously alive. Inevitably the links with its origins are no longer direct, but there has been a reconnection with contemporary traditional music in Scotland. The music of Scottish

Canadian musicians is known and enjoyed in Scotland, while Scottish musicians are often to be found in Canada.

Charles Dunn, who writes about Highland communities in Nova Scotia in his book *Highland Settler* (1953), quotes Malcolm Gillis from Margaree, Cape Breton. It is clear that maintaining the musical tradition was a matter of pride:

> When I was young and we went anywhere to visit, they'd be passing the pipes around from one young man to the next, and we'd all have to try a tune. Anyone who couldn't manage that would be so ashamed of himself, he'd try to learn pretty quick.

Gillis's forebears had come from Morar in the mid-nineteenth century, and Gillis himself evokes a community which successfully transplanted the language and the music and kept them alive.

When John Lorne Campbell visited the Maritimes in 1932, he estimated that there were about 50,000 Gaelic speakers. He met people whose families had come from Lewis, Harris, the Uists, Barra, Skye and Sutherland. There were eighteen to twenty congregations in Cape Breton holding services in Gaelic, and Gaelic singing contests were common. He found people able to sing traditional songs and versions of songs that were no longer current in Scotland.

Five years later, in Cape Breton again, he remarked on the 'strange incongruities' he encountered. It was 'a country where one can hear the Gaelic of Lewis, Skye or Barra against a seemingly most inappropriate background of dense spruce forest'. Here were Highland communities with no lairds, side by side with the Mi'kmaq; people referred to themselves as 'Lewismen' or 'Skyemen' and 'can describe perfectly, from their grandparents' reminiscing, places in the "Old Country" which they have never seen'. Among these communities 'an inherited nostalgia and old habits and customs have survived in a most astonishing way'. Several decades later, Margaret Bennett investigated the just-surviving Gaelic community in Newfoundland's Codroy Valley and was able to chronicle stories, songs and customs which had crossed the Atlantic from Glengarry and the Hebrides. The Codroy Valley settlers came to Newfoundland in the 1840s and '50s, some moving on from Nova Scotia where they found the best land already taken up.

Margaret Bennett identifies the sharing of music as a strikingly Highland feature:

> Exchanging a song or a tune is, for both peoples [Codroy Valley Scots and Highland Scots] as natural and spontaneous as sharing a piece of news, a favourite recipe, or an anecdote. It is part of everyday communication and has for countless centuries made a major and important contribution to the activities of the ceilidh.

The songs were also a crucial way of preserving the past as, like all folk song, they are a vehicle for oral history. They connect directly with people and events and activities. As in the Highlands, activities such as spinning and waulking or milling cloth – rhythmically beating the wet cloth to strengthen it – were accompanied by songs, though in the Codroy Valley these songs might be in French or English, as well as Gaelic. Irving Massey remembers the milling 'frolics' as they were called, from the 1970s in Antigonish County. (He also remembers tension between the Irish and Scottish communities.) The Highland music that survives now is divorced from the traditional life and work from which at one time it was inseparable, but it still contains memories of the past and links with the music's origins. The links become all the more important when the life has gone.

A strong impression of both the survival and the erosion of Gaelic tradition is present in Alistair MacLeod's fiction, which resonantly captures the past and present of Scottish communities in Cape Breton. His novel *No Great Mischief* (1999) centres on the '*clann Chalum Ruaidh*', the children of Red Calum, the harshness of life on the Cape Breton coast and the legacy of that harshness. He describes a group of people who are profoundly aware of their Scottish Highland roots but are also resolute survivors in an environment that was alien but familiar in its demands. And although the old Cape Breton communities are dispersing and traditions are vanishing, the need to come to terms with the fundamental claims of landscape and climate does not disappear, as many of MacLeod's stories illustrate.

Even in the 1930s John Lorne Campbell was commenting on abandoned houses and farms being repossessed by the forest. Charles Dunn quotes Duncan MacDonald who commented when he revisited his old Cape Breton homestead: 'It's a sad trial for me to come back to the ruins of the place where I was reared as a boy, tangled burdock is growing over it and tall nettles, and I can't get near the place.' People were leaving in significant numbers in the second half of the nineteenth century, to go west or to the United States, just as they left the Highlands, to cross the Atlantic or go south to Scotland's industrial heartland. Duncan MacDonald might be describing the experience of returning to an abandoned Highland steading. In MacLeod's stories the connection between Cape Breton and the Scottish Highlands, for all the incongruity that Lorne Campbell highlights, is reinforced by the echoes of displacement and abandonment. The crumbling stone of abandoned Cape Breton homes suggests Highland history repeating itself.

In a much earlier novel, *Barometer Rising* (1941), by another Scottish Canadian, Hugh MacLennan, a pipe band plays 'Lochaber No More' as the *Olympic* steams out of Halifax harbour. It is 1917 and the ship carries 5,000 Canadians going to war in Europe. Angus Murray is watching the ship's progress and listening to 'the lament the village pipers had played a hundred years ago when the clansmen who were the ancestors of half the people in Nova Scotia had left Scotland for the New World. Now Nova Scotian pipers were playing their men back to the Old World again.' While reflecting on the possibility that the music is no more than British propaganda, intended to inspire patriotism for the old country, he is moved in spite of himself – he is, after all, of Highland descent: 'he felt the music himself, felt his fingers clenched and a salty constriction behind his eyes'.

Music plays an important part in Alistair MacLeod's stories. In 'The Road to Rankin's Point', a family get-together inevitably means music. Out comes the fiddle, along with guitars and harmonicas, and the family play and sing. They all hold the fiddle bow in the same way and play in the same style 'older than any of our memories'. They do not think about the music: it just happens. In another MacLeod story, 'The Closing Down of Summer', the pipes and the fiddle are brought out for weddings and funerals. The story's Scottish Canadian characters turn to their musical tradition at times of stress or sadness. They sing 'the Gaelic songs remembered from our early youth'. Similarly, in the novel *No Great Mischief*, the funeral of one of the *clann Chalum ruaidh* would be unthinkable without fiddle and pipes. But we are also being told that these traditions are eroding. In 'The Tuning of Perfection', an elderly man who is 'the last of the authentic old-time Gaelic singers' is upset when a young woman sings a Gaelic lament too fast. She has no understanding of the words she sings. She has inherited the sounds without the meaning – and yet, there is meaning in the mere fact that the song lives.

In Sheldon Currie's novel *The Glace Bay Miners' Museum* (1995), set in a Cape Breton mining community, the heroine, Margaret MacNeil, meets Neil Currie, who opens a box 'full of brown sticks and a plaid bag': bagpipes. With the pipes, Gaelic-speaking Neil woos and wins Margaret, and reconnects her to a past which until now she has considered irrelevant. Neil says of his and Margaret's forebears, that when they left Scotland they 'lost their

tongues, their music, their songs. Everything but their shovels.'
The older generation still speaks some Gaelic, but to most of the
youngsters it is irrelevant. Neil is an exception, and loses his job
because he refuses to speak English to the foreman in the pit. In the
movie based on the novel, *Margaret's Museum*, there is a sequence
in which Margaret's mother gets impatient with the older men
who are sitting around drinking whisky and singing Gaelic songs.
In her eyes, the old ways have no place in a twentieth-century
industrial community. But music is seen as essential to Highland
identity. The family had settled originally in Mabou, on Cape
Breton's west coast, from where many left to work in the Glace
Bay coal mines. Leaving the land is seen as breaking an essential
connection, and the music leaves too. 'And the music?' asks one
of those who remained:

> Where is it now? They've all gone to work in the Glace Bay
> mines, the fiddlers, and the pipers, and the dancers, any that
> can walk at all and sober. They took the music with them.
> It's with them. It's not with us.

Going to work for wages is a kind of reversal. It abandons the
very thing that so many Scots gained when they came to Canada –
ownership of land and the independence that provides.

> If you have land, and a house on it, and a barn on it, and
> cows and chickens and all, nobody can lay you off, and you
> can always eat, poor as you might be, without getting to
> your knees for somebody's charity. Go, if you must, Morag,
> but keep your God, your tongue, your music and get some land.

The music just about survives, but everything else is lost.

  Cape Breton Road (2001), a novel by DR MacDonald, also
features the clash of the traditional and the contemporary. His

young hero, Innes Corbett, was born in Cape Breton but has grown up in the United States, so is doubly alienated from what survives of a Gaelic culture in the place of his birth. He feels out of place when he attends a dance and watches the dancers whirling to the music of a single fiddler, 'lean and brown and old like the instrument on his shoulder'. His uncle, with whom he is living, speaks Gaelic as a way of deliberately excluding him. Innes is reluctantly touched by the old ways, and goes to a Gaelic church service, which of course he cannot understand. When a psalm is sung the congregation, mostly elderly, mark the rhythm with their feet, 'a measured thump of hidden Sunday shoes', and Innes is affected in spite of himself:

> ... to Innes it was the rhythm of his axe, of his tree felling, this cadence of their singing. It echoed something deep in them that went a long way back, this foot beat, he could feel it even though he didn't know what it was and his foot was going, if lightly, discreetly, after all this was beyond him, before his time.

The rhythm of the axe is a Canadian rhythm, not a Scottish rhythm, and it is Innes's tree felling that links him with his Scottish Canadian heritage. It is, however, a heritage that he plans to escape in a very modern way, by growing cannabis and living on the proceeds, and by stealing a Cadillac in which to head west.

These novels tell us a great deal about how a Scottish Highland identity has survived its transplantation to Canada, and also about how it has changed and how the attitudes of the people it most affects also change. The novels of Margaret MacPhail, who in her eighties wrote fiction set a century earlier in the Bras D'Or Lake area, also document change. *Loch Bras D'Or* (1970) is the story of the MacNab family who came to Cape Breton from Barra in 1820. Two generations later, the family is dispersing and the old ways eroding. There is a strong ethnological vein in MacPhail's fiction as she records remembered ways of life and work in a Gaelic-speaking community and incorporates traditional stories, songs and beliefs.

Most of the Scots who settled in Cape Breton were Highlanders, so it is no surprise that it is the culture of the Gael that predominates there. But that culture has come to identify the Scot in a much more general way, throughout North America. Tartan and the bagpipes dominate the international image of Scotland. As Scottish communities became established in British North America many of them founded St Andrews, Caledonian and Highland societies, or societies taking their name from a specific Scottish place of origin. A key function of these societies was the support of needy Scots, helping newly-arrived immigrants with cash, information and advice, or just providing a point of contact for those who were adjusting to a new life. Many who in 1923 crossed the Atlantic on the *Metagama* sought out local Lewis societies, where they found familiar people and a familiar language. But commemoration and ritual were also features of these societies' activities, and tartan and music took on a symbolic importance. Their social gatherings were not complete without the pipes or the fiddle, which had quickly established themselves as cultural icons. Sir George Simpson travelling through the Hudson's Bay Company domain took his piper with him. In the most lonely outposts there was a good chance that any group of even the most hard-bitten wilderness men could produce a fiddle to bring in the new year, or just to pass the time.

Music making could be in the form of impromptu ceilidhs, the spontaneous eruption of music and story-telling when people got together (the original meaning of the Gaelic word *ceilidh* is 'visit') – or of grander occasions, like the first ball of the Aberdeen, Banff and Kincardineshire Association of Winnipeg, which had begun life as the Fraserburgh Society. The ball took place in December 1911 and was reported in the *Aberdeen Journal*, which suggests the sense of connection with absent Scots. 'The atmosphere of the large ballroom,' it said, 'was distinctly Scottish.' The association at this time had a membership of 220, which included 'almost every native of Fraserburgh and district'. Also consistently celebrated was the poetry of Robert Burns, which acted as a unifying factor in any gathering of Scots, Highland or Lowland. Burns Night (25 January), St Andrew's Day (30 November) and Hogmanay were key dates in the calendars of Scottish societies. Burns, of course, was not a Highlander. His poetry was rooted in Lowland rural traditions and the Ayrshire in which he grew up. His poems came to British North America with Lowland emigrants, and editions of Burns sold well throughout North America. Burns became absorbed into a generalised Scottish identity, as he was in Scotland and throughout the world, with Highland tartan and bagpipes becoming essential features of Burns night celebrations. One of the ways in which the hero of Frederick Niven's *The Transplanted* demonstrates his Scottishness is through Burns: 'on Burns Nicht the Scotsmen of the valley always had him in the chair'.

In the 1840s there was a proliferation of Highland societies in the Maritimes, linked with the original Highland Society founded in London in 1778. These combined the promotion of good agricultural practice, support for those in need and the preservation of what were identified as traditional Highland manners and customs. Again, the pipes and tartan became icons with which all Scots were happy to identify. It was in the nature of these societies that historic frictions between Highland and Lowland, and the more recent collapse of the clan system which had sent so many thousands into exile, were not in the foreground. An idealised version of the clan emerged alongside a heroic image of a martial past. Although it suited many Scots to sign up to this, especially as it provided an easy and often enjoyable way of maintaining a Scottish identity, there were those who did not so readily overlook the circumstances that had brought their lives in Scotland to an end. These were remembered in vivid and uncompromising Gaelic poetry, often celebrating their new country while evoking the injustices of the old. Others wrote with profound and emotionally-charged regret of the Highlands they had left.

John 'The Hunter' MacDonald, who left Lochaber for Cape Breton in 1834, expressed his sense of loss in 'Song for America': 'Alas, Lord, that I did not die before I left Scotland, before I turned my back on my dear homeland and thereby lost my vigour.' But Allan MacDonald, who had settled in Antigonish County eighteen years earlier, took a different view. 'The land you left is a land without kindness, a land without respect for tenants... it is not fitting to disprise the land of promise where they are now respected men.' If Michael MacDonald from South Uist could write of Prince Edward Island, 'Fair is the place I have here by the sea', and Ann Gillis, who was among the first settlers in Glengarry County, felt she had arrived in 'the land of contentment', John MacDonald was not alone in viewing the leaving of Scotland as a terrible mistake. One of the most famous Gaelic laments was written by John Maclean from Tiree, who settled first in Pictou County and then moved to Antigonish. In his poem 'The Gloomy Forest' he writes, 'I soon discovered that far-away fields are not so green as reported'.

Lowland poets expressed a similar ambivalence. Andrew Wanless from Berwickshire, who emigrated to Toronto in 1851, writes in his poem 'Our Mither Tongue':

> We'll ne'er forget that glorious land,
> Where Scott and Burns are sung;
> Their songs are printed on our hearts
> In our auld mither tongue.

And Thomas Laidlaw, who became president of the Guelph St Andrews Society, writes in 'The Old Scottish Songs':

O, sing us to-night from the old Scottish songs –
The songs which our mothers would hear
In the old cottage homes, that were covered with thatch,
In a land that will ever be dear.

But Alexander McLachlan, born in Renfrewshire in 1820, is quite clear about where his loyalties lie.

Hurrah! For the grand old forest land
Where Freedom spreads her pinion;
Hurrah! With me, for the maple tree,
Hurrah! For the New Dominion.

And Alexander Wingfield from Blantyre, who as a boy worked in a Glasgow cotton factory, celebrates Canada as 'the only land/Whose sons are truly free'.

Clearly, individual experiences varied, on both sides of the Atlantic. But even those who felt most positively about their new lives in Canada did not necessarily want to lose their Scottishness, nor did it seem that becoming Canadian required that. Indeed, as the many Scottish societies suggest, the more deep-rooted the transplantation, the more important it became not just to preserve a Scottish identity (which might not have much to do with an individual's personal origins), but to maintain links with other Scots. An important part of the role of Scottish societies in Canada was to look after their own, in a way that might not have seemed appropriate or necessary in the old country.

Many Highland societies, as well as promoting Highland music and dancing, became the focus of Highland sporting activities. Shinty came to Canada with the Scots, and out of it was born ice hockey. In his novel *Glengarry School Days* Ralph Connor describes a mid-nineteenth century game of 'shinny' played on ice, and likens it to Highland warfare. A piece in the *Celtic Monthly* of July 1893, signed 'Sgian Dubh', indicates how summer sports took over from winter meetings:

> The arena is changed from the platform and the hall to the green sward, where the bagpipes are heard cheering on the shinty players, providing music for the skilled dancer, or in martial strain striving for a prize in keen competition. The Highland games of Canada are noted events. Their fame is well known in Scotland and all over this vast continent.

The piece goes on to say that the programme 'varies but little from that of the gatherings in the Highlands', featuring 'Highland dances, bagpiping, Highland costume, putting the stone, tossing the caber, vaulting, jumping' and sometimes quoits, bowling, shinty and tugs-of-war. 'Sgian Dubh' comments: 'The national sentiment is stimulated, and the best phases of our national character are the more easily reached and cultivated because of the manly exercises and the games of the old home being kept alive.' It is unclear whether 'national' means Canadian or Scottish; perhaps it means both, and suggests that the two are inseparable.

These events were primarily for those who identified themselves as being of Scottish origin, but they were also spectacles that could hardly fail to impinge on whatever community hosted them. A tongue-in-cheek announcement in a Vancouver newspaper indicates the high public profile of Scottish activities:

> We announce that the pipe band will start at 11 o'clock from Hastings Street for the Caledonian gathering at the park; we make this announcement in order that ordinary citizens who are not Scotch may take to the woods.

Behind the good-humoured confidence expressed here, is the

assumption that Scottish Canadians do not have to explain themselves or apologise. Everyone knows who they are. Back in Scotland the pipe band and Highland games played their part in masking and defusing ancient and not so ancient hostility and injustice, and this is echoed in the way a unified Scottish identity is celebrated in Canada. But not all Scottish Canadians saw things in such straightforward terms. Wilfred Campbell in his *The Scotsman in Canada* (1912) reflected: 'men may rave of the heather, the hills, the pibroch, and the Brig of Ayr [a Burns icon], but all the time the real Scotland and the true Scottish people are a mystery to themselves and to others'. It seems a very modern comment, implying as it does the complexity of Scotland's history. And Wilfred Campbell sees Canada's history as closely tied to that of Scotland.

Highland games and Scottish festivals today flourish all over Canada. A selective list of such events in the summer of 2003 includes games at Glengarry, Sarnia, Chatham and Fergus, Ontario; in Alberta the High River, Grande Prairie, Calgary, Edmonton, Canmore and Red Deer Highland Games and an Annual Highland Happening also at Red Deer; games at Penticton and Coquitlam in British Columbia; the New Brunswick Highland Games; the Antigonish games and the Celtic Colours International Festival in Nova Scotia; the Canadian Highland Dance Championships. Participating are music societies, pipe bands and dance troupes (the Antigonish Highland Society pipe band, for example, and the Scotia Highland Dancers) as well as sportsmen and women. They are focal points for the celebration of all things Scottish, some authentic, some invented, but all with an unmistakable Scottish identity.

In the early decades of emigration, most Scots who came to British North America settled into rural lives. They were farmers, sometimes fishermen or lumbermen, but their livelihoods depended on the land. When mineral resources began to be exploited and mining developed, many Scots were involved, and they depended on the land in a rather different way. They worked underground rather than on the ground. Others came in response to the needs of settlements for skills and trades; women, often single, came to take up domestic positions. Emigration agents often specified what was being looked for. As cities and industries evolved, the nature of the labour force changed and in Canada, as in Europe, there was a move to the urban centres. There was also a move from eastern Canada to the west, as the agricultural potential of the prairie provinces was exploited and first the railways and then the motor car revolutionised transport. And thousands of Scottish Canadians crossed the American border to work in Boston, Detroit and other cities that offered employment and good wages. The Scots who had settled in Nova Scotia and New Brunswick, the territory that, for all its massive forests, was most like their homeland, began to leave. New migrations began, which still continue.

Contemporary Scottish Canadian writers are much concerned with this process, and their own lives reflect it. Hugh MacLennan was born in the coal-mining community of Glace Bay in Cape Breton, the same community featured in Sheldon Currie's novel, but spent most of his writing and teaching career in Montreal. *Barometer Rising*, his first novel, draws more directly on his Cape Breton background than his later fiction. His characters relate in different ways to their Highland origins, aware that with each generation the links grow more tenuous. Alistair MacLeod was also born in Cape Breton, in a rural community near Inverness; his grandfather worked in a coal mine. He, too, went west, but clearly stays closely in touch with his Cape Breton and Highland inheritance. His stories almost without exception explore the extent to which it is possible to keep that inheritance alive. Margaret Laurence's Morag Gunn, in *The Diviners*, goes east to Toronto and then to England, as Laurence herself did, and then west again, although not back to her Manitoba birthplace, which is a fictionalised version of her creator's birthplace, Neepawa.

Morag, with the help of her guardian Christie Logan, re-invents her Highland identity, but when she has the chance to confirm it, by returning to the Sutherland homeland, she realises that it is no longer necessary. What matters is her identity as a Canadian, however Scottish that may be, and her Manitoba origins.

In a nation of displaced peoples this re-examination of connections and relationships with the past is part of life, as it is in a nation – Scotland – that has seen so many people leave. Many Scottish Canadians are visiting Scotland in order to trace their origins, and there is a growing number of institutions and events in Scotland that reflect that interest. In 1999 Orkney welcomed Canadians to the Orkney Homecoming. Many of those who attended were the descendants of Hudson's Bay Company employees who had made their homes in Canada. The SEALLAM! Visitor Centre at Northton, Harris, houses *Co leis thu?*, a genealogical research project which has already amassed a huge amount of information about families who left the Hebrides. (*Co leis thu?* is the question that Innes Corbett, in DR MacDonald's novel, is asked by the old people in Cape Breton: whose are you? To whom do you belong?)

At Edinburgh's Museum of Scotland there is a display devoted to emigration, which includes Canada, and in 2003 a major exhibition 'Trailblazers – Scots in Canada' told the story of Scottish Canadians, assembling material from both sides of the Atlantic. An exhibition at the McCord Museum in Montreal looked at the Scots and the French in Quebec. Many smaller museums around Scotland contain material that relates directly to the Scots who went to Canada. The National Library of Scotland has an extensive collection relating to emigration and settlement in Canada, and many libraries around Scotland can help with genealogical enquiries.

Hugh MacLennan came to Scotland in 1958 and wrote about the experience in an essay called 'Scotchman's Return'. His family had come from Kintail in the West Highlands between Fort William and Skye. He describes his father, a doctor, as typically Scottish – or 'Scotch', in the word his father preferred.

> All the perplexity and doggedness of the race was in him, its loneliness, tenderness and affection, its deceptive vitality, its quick flashes of violence, its dog-whistle sensitivity to sounds to which Anglo-Saxons are stone deaf...

Many of these traits emerge in the Scottish characters to be found in MacLennan's fiction.

His visit to Kintail prompted a comparison with the vast empty spaces of Canada, and he highlights an essential difference. Unlike Canada's wilderness, the empty spaces of the Highlands once were populated: 'in a deserted Highland glen you feel that everyone who ever mattered is dead and gone... They are haunted by the lost loves and passions of a thousand years.'

Nearly forty years later the Canadian poet Stephen Scobie made a visit to the country of his birth. He grew up in Glasgow and went to Canada in 1965 at the age of twenty-one. Although he had returned to Scotland several times before, this particular trip was planned as a 'private rediscovery', which he writes about in his *Taking the Gate: A Journey through Scotland* (1996). 'To *re*-visit a place is to honour its claims on your memory,' he writes, and that is as true of those who re-visit several generations after departure. He weaves poems through his account of his visit, and the first of these is an affectionately critical picture of a country which spits out its people 'in a desperate diaspora/all over the world':

> Clearing the land, clearing its throat
>
> As if it had a sheep stuck in its tonsils,
> clogged with wool, washed

down with whisky.

Dark little island, dark little
half of an island:
lochs and glens and leaking castles,

rain in August, rain in July,
kilts and umbrellas the national dress.

Scobie's is a very personal journey, but the Scotland he
rediscovers is one that would be recognised by most Scots and most
returning Scottish Canadians, perhaps not in every detail but in its
inescapable features: mountains and lochs, rain and mist, wind,
harbours and shores, uncompromising castles, football, kilts. But
memory and rediscovery are about people, and meeting again with
family and friends, and encountering new people. Scots living their
lives in Scotland today are part of the process, as are the thousands
of Scottish Canadians looking for their place in Scotland's as well
as Canada's history.

In 1999, the same year as the Orkney Homecoming, the National
Museums of Scotland took a small display called 'The Emigrant's
Kist' to British Columbia. Its centrepiece was a kist, or chest, of the
kind that so many emigrant families took with them, packed with
their belongings. The display's kist was also packed with examples
of these: a few clothes, a shawl, a blanket, a bible, essential domestic
utensils and sewing materials, some tools, perhaps a treasured item
of jewellery, a set of bagpipes, a fiddle. Most people left Scotland
with very little, not least because their possessions were few. With
the kist were a few panels explaining the background to emigration
to Canada and outlining the story of where Scots went and what
they did.

After a spell in Victoria on Vancouver Island and Vancouver the
display moved east to Winnipeg before continuing on to Ontario and

Quebec. It made a final appearance at the McCord Museum before returning home. Everywhere it went it has generated great interest. Although it is specifically about the Scots who went to Canada, it also represents the emigrant experience as a whole. Displacement and exile, transplantation and new beginnings, are a part of the history of hundreds of thousands of people.

Two years after 'The Emigrant's Kist' crossed the Atlantic, another kist took its place in a similar National Museums display that spent a year travelling around the Scottish Highlands and Islands. This exhibit, called 'Home and Away', focused on those who left the Highlands and those who are now returning in search of their roots. It, too, generated great interest, both among Highland communities, where so many families have Canadian connections, and among visitors to those communities. It reminded Scots that for centuries departure has been a part of Scottish history, and that without these departures those nations that began as British colonies would themselves have very different histories. Now homecoming is equally a part of the history of both Scotland and Canada.

Over a century ago there was a homecoming of a rather different kind. For many generations the Dewars of Strathfillan, between Killin and Crianlarich in Perthshire, had been hereditary keepers of objects connected with St Fillan, an Irish missionary in the Highlands in the eighth century. The most valued of these objects was a beautifully decorated silver crozier, which is said to have been in Robert the Bruce's tent on the eve of the Battle of Bannockburn in 1314. In 1818 Archibald Dewar, hereditary keeper at the time, emigrated to Upper Canada and took the crozier with him. The Dewars had a struggle to establish themselves and made several moves in their effort to farm successfully. In 1853 Daniel Wilson left Edinburgh to take up a position as professor of history and literature at the University College of Toronto. He already had a distinguished reputation as an antiquarian and archaeologist, and as a member of the Society of Antiquaries of Scotland was responsible for re-organising their museum. His younger brother George was the first director of what became the Museum of Science and Art in Edinburgh, now the Royal Museum. (The two museums came together in 1985 to form the core of the National Museums of Scotland.) Daniel Wilson knew Sir George Simpson, and it was through this contact that George persuaded officers of the Hudson's Bay Company to collect Native material to send back to Scotland.

It was not only Native material that came to Edinburgh. Daniel Wilson had since the 1840s been investigating the whereabouts of St Fillan's crozier, and when he was in Canada he finally tracked it down. In 1877 he arranged to purchase it and send it back to Scotland, where it joined the collections of the Antiquities Museum and is now a key exhibit in the Museum of Scotland. The story has a final chapter which would have pleased Sir Daniel, who was knighted in 1880 for his services to Canadian education. When the National Museums of Scotland were fundraising for the Museum of Scotland, the descendants of the Dewars, still living in Ontario, returned the purchase price of the crozier as a donation. They were present at the opening of the new museum in 1998. This beautiful and intricately decorated object, an immensely significant part of Scotland's medieval heritage, is also a symbol of the Scottish-Canadian connection.

Emigration imprinted Shetland, as it did every other part of Scotland. This chapter opens with some lines from a poem written in Shetland dialect by Christine De Luca, a Shetlander married to a descendant of Italian immigrants (a reminder that Scotland is a nation of immigrants as well as emigrants). 'Completin da Circle' tells of emigration and of return. It touches on the story of a younger generation who left and remained, to produce children who are 'true Canadians', expressing their Canadian identity through their inheritance of Scottish tradition: they wear the kilt,

and demonstrate the sword dance to the folk back home in the old
country, completing the circle.

> We nivver kent why you cam back fae Winnipeg
> In sepia photos you lookit weel set up, ice skates
> owre da airm, fur cep: a Shetland joiner wi a taste
> fur stivvenin winters and skyscraper pay. Some said
> you fell or lost a poase or hed ill luck in love
> Something brook you, browt you silent hame. Some
> plenishin man still be dere, sae gud your haands
> Chance returned a grandson ta pick up da treed
> an waeve hit in. His bairns ir true Canadians
> Dey wear da kilt an proudly shaa wis foo ta dö
> da sword dance, mak a saltire on da flör, step
> neatly roond hits quarters ta complete da circle.

Map 1: Scotland

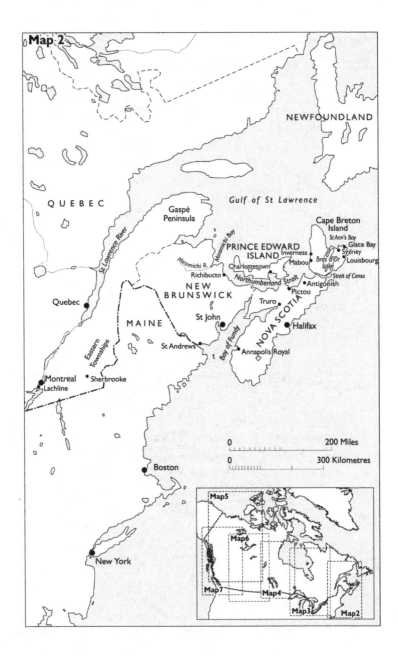

Map 2

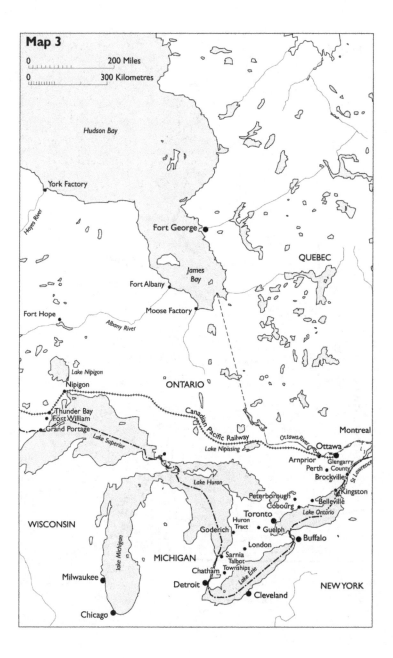

Map 3

0   200 Miles

0   300 Kilometres

Hudson Bay

York Factory

Hayes River

Fort George

QUEBEC

James Bay

Fort Albany

Moose Factory

Fort Hope

Albany River

Lake Nipigon

ONTARIO

Nipigon

Thunder Bay
Fort William
Grand Portage

Canadian Pacific Railway

Lake Superior

Lake Nipissing

Ottawa River

Montreal

Ottawa

Arnprior
Perth   Glengarry County

Brockville

St Lawrence

Kingston

Lake Huron

Peterborough

Belleville

Cobourg

Lake Ontario

Toronto

WISCONSIN

Lake Michigan

Goderich

Huron Tract

Guelph

Buffalo

London

MICHIGAN

Sarnia
Talbot Townships

Milwaukee

Chatham

Lake Erie

Detroit

Cleveland

NEW YORK

Chicago

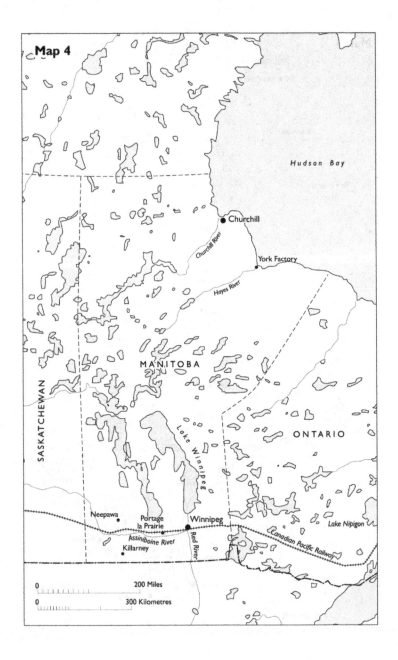

Map 4

Hudson Bay

Churchill

Churchill River

York Factory

Hayes River

MANITOBA

SASKATCHEWAN

Lake Winnipeg

ONTARIO

Neepawa

Portage
la Prairie

Winnipeg

Lake Nipigon

Assiniboine River

Red River

Canadian Pacific Railway

Killarney

0   200 Miles

0   300 Kilometres

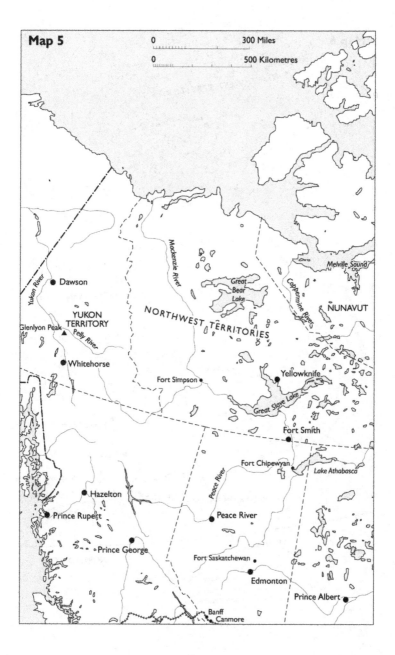

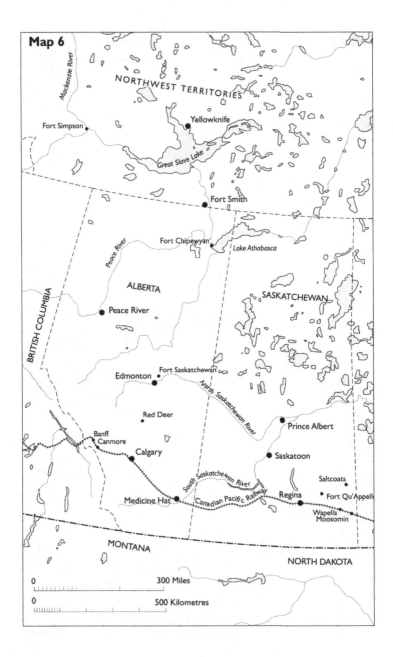

Map 6

NORTHWEST TERRITORIES

Mackenzie River

Fort Simpson

Yellowknife

Great Slave Lake

Fort Smith

Peace River

Fort Chipewyan

Lake Athabasca

ALBERTA

SASKATCHEWAN

BRITISH COLUMBIA

Peace River

Edmonton

Fort Saskatchewan

North Saskatchewan River

Red Deer

Prince Albert

Banff
Canmore

Calgary

Saskatoon

South Saskatchewan River

Saltcoats

Medicine Hat

Canadian Pacific Railway

Regina

Fort Qu'Appelle

Wapella
Moosomin

MONTANA

NORTH DAKOTA

| 0 | 300 Miles |
| 0 | 500 Kilometres |

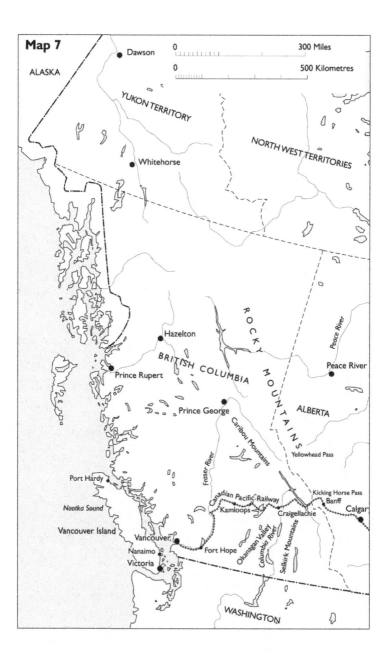

Map 7

ALASKA

Dawson

0 ⎯⎯⎯⎯⎯⎯⎯ 300 Miles

0 ⎯⎯⎯⎯⎯⎯⎯ 500 Kilometres

YUKON TERRITORY

NORTH WEST TERRITORIES

Whitehorse

Hazelton

ROCKY

Peace River

BRITISH COLUMBIA

MOUNTAINS

Prince Rupert

Prince George

ALBERTA

Caribou Mountains

Fraser River

Yellowhead Pass

Port Hardy

Canadian Pacific Railway

Kicking Horse Pass

Banff

Nootka Sound

Kamloops

Craigellachie

Calgary

Vancouver Island

Vancouver

Fort Hope

Nanaimo

Victoria

Okanagan Valley

Columbia River

Selkirk Mountains

WASHINGTON

Chronology

1775	Royal Highland Emigrants regiment raised to fight for British in American War of Independence
1779	North West Company founded
1781	British surrender at Yorktown ends American War of Independence
1784	Cape Breton and New Brunswick become provinces
1785	Beaver Club founded
1788	Alexander Mackenzie expedition reaches Beaufort Sea
1791	Division of Upper and Lower Canada
1792	Glengarry settlement founded, Upper Canada
1993	Alexander Mackenzie expedition reaches Pacific coast
1803	Passenger Act Settlement in PEI organised by Lord Selkirk
1808	Simon Fraser expedition down Fraser River
1812	First emigration to Red River organised by Lord Selkirk USA invades British North America
1813	Second emigration to Red River organised by Lord Selkirk
1815	Bathurst Plan
1816	Battle of Seven Oaks, Red River Town of Galt founded by William Dickson in Upper Canada
1817	Norman MacLeod and his followers arrive at Pictou, NS
1818	Arctic expedition led by John Ross
1819	Arctic expeditions led by William Parry and John Franklin
1820	John A MacDonald, future first prime minister, arrives in Canada Emigration societies begin to be founded in Scottish Lowlands
1821	HBC and NWC merge
1825	Alexander Macnab founds township, Upper Canada Erie Canal completed

Second Arctic expedition led by John Franklin
1826   Canada Company formed
        Glasgow Colonial Society founded
        George Simpson governor of Hudson's Bay Company
1827   Town of Guelph founded
1828   Cuthbert Grant appointed Warden of the Plains
        First agent-general for emigration appointed by
            colonial government
1831   Quarantine Station established at Grosse Ile
        New Brunswick and Nova Scotia Company formed
1832   UK Reform Act
1833   British American Land Co acquire 850,000 acres in
            Lower Canada – the Eastern Townships
1837   Radical rebellion led by William Lyon Mackenzie
1838   Donald Smith joins HBC
1839   Durham Report recommends Responsible Government
1840   Colonial Land and Emigration Commission reports
1842   James Douglas supervises building of Fort Victoria,
        Vancouver Island
1843   Disruption of Church of Scotland
        George Brown founds the Toronto *Globe*
1845   Third Arctic expedition led by John Franklin
1846   Oregon Treaty gives Oregon and Washington to USA
        Failure of potato crop in Scotland
1847   Lord Elgin becomes governor-general of British North
        America
1851   HBC sells Vancouver Island holdings for settlement
        James Douglas becomes governor
        Emigration Advancement Act
        Gordon of Cluny expels tenants from Barra, South
        Uist and Benbecula
1857   John A Macdonald becomes prime minister of British
        North America

	Expedition led by John Palliser to survey potential railway route through Rocky Mountains
1858	Gold discovered on Thompson River
1864	1st British Columbia legislative council
1867	British North American Act provides for Confederation of Ontario, Quebec, Nova Scotia and New Brunswick
1869	HBC gives up chartered rights
	First Riel Rebellion
1870	Manitoba joins Confederation
1872	Dominion Lands Act
	Immigration and Colonisation Act
	Fleming and Grant survey for Canadian Pacific Railway
1873	Alexander Mackenzie becomes 1st Liberal prime minister of Canada
1880	Canadian Pacific Railway Company formed
1883	Napier Commission appointed to investigate conditions of Highland crofters
1885	Second Riel Rebellion
	Completion of CPR
1886	Crofters' Holdings Act
1897	Northwest Territories becomes province of Canada
1905	Alberta and Saskatchewan becomes provinces
1922	Empire Settlement Act
1923	*Metagama* sails from Lewis with settlers for Ontario
1924	*Marloch* sails from North Uist with settlers for Alberta
1935	John Buchan becomes governor-general of Canada

Places to Visit

Scotland

EVIDENCE OF THE place of emigration in Scotland's history can be found in small museums and heritage sites all over the country. Try **www.scottishmuseums.org.uk** for information on local museums: a small selection is mentioned below. The **Museum of Scotland** in Edinburgh has a gallery on emigration and Scots abroad called 'Scotland and the World' which includes Canadian material. Its temporary exhibition 'Trailblazers – Scots in Canada' ran from October 2003 to January 2004 in the **Royal Museum** next door, where there is a permanent exhibition of Native North American artefacts. The **National War Museum** in Edinburgh Castle has displays relating to Scottish regiments involved in North American wars. The **Scottish National Portrait Gallery** contains portraits of some of the people mentioned in this book.

The **People's Palace** museum in Glasgow and the **McLean Museum** in Greenock have material related to the Clyde's connections with North America. The **Stromness Museum** in Orkney has displays on the Hudson's Bay Company. Many museums display material connected with departures from Scotland and their context, for example the **Highland Folk Museum**, Kingussie; **Timespan**, Helmsdale; **Cromarty Courthouse Museum; Forres Museum**. For archive and genealogical material visit the **Scottish National Archive** and the **National Library of Scotland**, both in Edinburgh. The **SEALLAM! Visitor Centre**, Northton, Harris, focuses on material relating to emigration from the Western Isles and has a wealth of genealogical information.

Canada

MOST OF CANADA's history museums include material directly related to immigration, among which there is likely to be material relevant to the Scottish Canadian experience. Important collections are held at Toronto's **Royal Ontario Museum**, Ottawa's **Museum of Civilisation**, the **McCord Museum** in Montreal, the **Manitoba Museum of Man and Nature**, Winnipeg and the **Royal British Columbia Museum**, Victoria. Winnipeg is also the home of the **Hudson's Bay Company Archive**.

For information on the wealth of museums, historic sites, heritage centres and archives relevant to pioneer settlement, farming, the fur trade, mining, shipping and railways try www. virtualmuseum.ca. Here is a small selection from the many hundreds listed: the **Nova Scotia Museum**, Halifax and the **Halifax Citadel National Historic Site**; the **Highland Village** at Lake Bras d'Or; **Antigonish Heritage Museum**; the **Hector Centre**, Pictou; the **Glengarry Pioneer Museum**; the **Guelph Civic Museum**; **Mackenzie House**, Toronto (the home of William Lyon Mackenzie); **Sevenoaks House Museum, Lower Fort Garry National Historic Site** and **La Musée de St Boniface**, all near Winnipeg; the **Margaret Laurence Home**, Neepawa, Manitoba, **Glenbow Museum**, Calgary; **Fort Chipewyan Bicentennial Museum** (one of several Hudson's Bay Company historic sites); the **Western Development Museum** at four sites in Saskatchewan – Moose Jaw, Saskatoon, North Battlefield and Yorkton; **Vancouver Museum; Craigdarroch House**, near Victoria (the home of Robert Dunsmuir).

Bibliography

Included in this list are all the books referred to in the text, and other relevant sources.

Adams, Ian and Somerville, Meredyth: *Cargoes of Despair and Hope*, Edinburgh, 1993

Allison, Susan: *A Pioneer Gentlewoman in British Columbia*, ed Margaret A Ormsby, Vancouver, 1991

Atwood, Margaret: *Survival, a Thematic Guide to Canadian Literature*, Toronto, 1972

Ballantyne, RM: *Hudson's Bay, or Every-day Life in the Wilds of North America*, London, 1848
—*Away in the Wilderness, or Life among the Red Indians and Fur-Traders of North America*, 1877
—*The Iron Horse, or Life on the Line*, London, 1848

Bell, William: *Hints to Emigrants in a Series of Letters from Upper Canada*, Edinburgh, 1824

Bennett, Margaret: *The Last Stronghold: Scottish Gaelic Traditions of Newfoundland*, Edinburgh, 1989
—*Oatmeal and the Catechism: Scottish Settlers in Quebec*, Edinburgh, 1998

Brebner, B: *Canada: A Modern History*, Ann Arbor, 1960

Bryce, George: *The Scotsman in Canada* Vol II. *Western Canada*, London, 1911

Buchan, John: *Memory Hold-the-door*, London, 1940
—*Sick Heart River*, London, 1941

Bumsted, JF: *The Scots in Canada*, Ottawa, 1982
—*The People's Clearance: Highland Emigration to British North America 1775–1815*, Edinburgh, 1982
—(ed) *Collected Writings of Lord Selkirk 1810–20*, Winnipeg, 1988

Cage, RA (ed): *The Scots Abroad 1750–1914*, London, 1985

Calder, Jenni (ed): *The Enterprising Scot*, Edinburgh, 1986
—(ed) *No Ordinary Journey*, Edinburgh, 1993

—(ed) *Present Poets 2: Scotland to the World to Scotland*, Edinburgh, 1999

Campbell, D and MacLean, RA: *Beyond the Atlantic Roar, a study of the Nova Scotia Scots*, Toronto, 1974

Campbell, John Lorne: *Songs Remembered in Exile*, Edinburgh, 1999

Campbell, Wilfred: *The Scotsman in Canada* Vol 1 *Eastern Canada*, London, 1912

Campey, Lucille H: *A Very Fine Class of Immigrants*, Toronto, 2001
—'*Fast Sailing and Copper Bottomed': Aberdeen Sailing Ships and the Emigrant Scots They Carried to Canada*, Toronto, 2002

Clark, Daniel (ed): *Selections from Scottish Canadian Poets*, Toronto, 1909

Connor, Ralph: *Glengarry School Days*, Toronto, 1902

Currie, Sheldon: *The Glace Bay Miners' Museum*, Wreck Cove, 1995

Devine, TM (ed): *Scottish Emigration and Scottish Society*, Edinburgh, 1992
—*The Scottish Nation*, London, 1999

Dobson, David: *Ships from Scotland to America 1628–1828*, Baltimore, 1998

Dunn, Charles W: *Highland Settler: A Portrait of the Scottish Gael in Nova Scotia*, Toronto, 1953

Fairley, Margaret (ed): *Selected Writings of William Lyon Mackenzie 1824 to 1837*, Toronto, 1960

Fergusson, Adam: *Practical Notes Made During a Tour in Canada*, Edinburgh, 1833

Fleming, Rae (ed): *The Lochaber Emigrants to Glengarry*, Toronto, 1994

Fry, Michael: *The Scottish Empire*, Edinburgh, 2002

Galbraith, JK: *Made to Last*, London, 1964

Galt, John: *Bogle Corbet or the Emigrants*, London 1831
—*Lawrie Todd or Settlers in the Woods*, London, 1832
—*Autobiography of John Galt*, 1833

Gray, JM: *Lord Selkirk of the Red River*, London, 1963

Green, Lorne: *Chief Engineer: Life of a Nation Builder*, Toronto, 1993

Harper, Marjory: *Adventurers and Exiles: The Great Scottish Exodus*, London, 2003

Harper, Marjorie and Vance, Michael (eds): *Myth, Migration and the Making of Memory, Scotia and Nova Scotia c.1700–1990*, Halifax and Edinburgh, 1999

Hill, Douglas: *Great Migrations I: The Scots to Canada*, London, 1972

Howison, John: *Sketches of Upper Canada*, Edinburgh, 1825

Hunter, James: *A Dance Called America*, Edinburgh, 1994
—*Glencoe and the Indians*, Edinburgh, 1996

Kerrigan, Catherine (ed): *The Immigrant Experience*, Guelph, 1992
Laurence, Margaret: *A Bird in the House*, Toronto, 1963
—*A Jest of God*, Toronto, 1966
—*The Diviners*, London, 1974

Little, JI: *Crofters and Habitants, settler society, economy and culture in a Quebec township, 1848–1881*, Montreal, 1991

MacDonald, DR: *Cape Breton Road*, London, 2001

Macdonald, Norman: *Canada: Immigration and Colonisation 1841–1903*, Toronto, 1966

McDonnell, Margaret: *The Emigrant Experience: Songs of Highland Emigrants in North America*, Toronto, 1982

MacDougall, Robert: *The Emigrant's Guide to North America*, ed Elizabeth Thompson, Toronto, 1998

Macinnes, Allan I, Harper, Marjory-Ann D and Fryer, Linda G (eds): *Scotland and the Americas, c.1650–c.1939: A Documentary Source Book*, Edinburgh, 2002

MacKay, Donald: *Scotland Farewell: The People of the Hector*, Toronto, 1996

Mackenzie, George A (ed): *From Aberdeen to Ottawa in 1845: The Diary of Alexander Muir*, Aberdeen, 1990

McLean, Marianne: *The People of Glengarry: Highlanders in Transition 1745–1820*, Montreal, 1991

Maclean, Rory: *The Oatmeal Ark*, London, 1997

MacLennan, Hugh: —*Barometer Rising*, Toronto, 1941
—*Cross-Country*, Toronto, 1958
—*Scotchman's Return and Other Essays*, New York, 1960
—*Seven Rivers of Canada*, Toronto, 1977

MacLeod, Alistair: *No Great Mischief*, London, 1999
—*Island*, London, 2002

MacLeod, Margaret A (ed): *The Letters of Letitia Hargrave*, Toronto, 1947

McLeod, Mona: *Leaving Scotland*, Edinburgh, 1996

MacNeil, Neil: *Highland Heart in Nova Scotia*, New York, 1948

McPhail, Margaret: *Loch Bras d'Or*, Windsor, 1972

Moodie, Susanna: *Roughing it in the Bush*, Toronto, 1962

—*Life in the Clearings versus the Bush*, Toronto, 1959

Munro, Alice: *Friend of My Youth*, London, 1991
—*Open Secrets*, London, 1994

Newman, Peter C: *Company of Adventurers*, Markham, 1985
—*Caesars of the Wilderness*, Markham, 1987
—*Merchant Princes*, Markham, 1991

Niven, Frederick John: *The Flying Years*, London, 1935
—*The Transplanted*, London, 1944

Norton, Wayne: *Help Us to a Better Land: Crofter Colonies in the Prairie West*, Regina, 1994

Pennant, Thomas: *Tour of Scotland and a Voyage to the Hebrides*, London, 1773

Rae, William Fraser: *Newfoundland to Manitoba*, London, 1881

Rattray, WJ: *The Scot in British North America*, 4 vols, Toronto, 1880–84

Reid, W S (ed): *The Scottish Tradition in Canada*, Toronto, 1976

Richards, Eric: *The Highland Clearances*, Edinburgh, 2000

Ross, Eric: *Beyond the River and the Bay*, Toronto, 1970

Scobie, Stephen: *Taking the Gate: A Journey through Scotland*, Red Deer, 1996

Story, Norah: *Oxford Companion to Canadian History and Literature*, Toronto, 1973

Traill, Catherine Parr: *Lost in the Backwoods*, 1882
—*The Female Emigrant's Guide and Hints on Canadian Housekeeping*, Toronto, 1854

Wilkie, J: *Metagama, a journey from Lewis to the New World*, Edinburgh, 1987

Acknowledgements

THIS BOOK GREW out of the work I did as Head of Museum of Scotland International at the National Museums of Scotland. During that time the NMS exhibition 'Trailblazers – Scots in Canada' began to take shape. It opened at the Royal Museum, Edinburgh in October 2003. This book owes a great deal to the enthusiasm and generosity in sharing knowledge of former colleagues Maureen Barrie, Hugh Cheape, George Dalgleish and David Forsyth: heartfelt thanks to them all.

My thanks also to Susan Manning and Alex Murdoch, partners in the 'big idea' which set me on the road to writing about Scots in North America, to Jim Hunter, to Irving Massey, to Christine De Luca for permission to quote in full her poem 'Completin da Circle', and to Carcanet Press for permission to quote from Iain Crichton Smith's 'The Exiles'. I am grateful to Jim Lewis for drawing the maps and to Jennie Renton for her sympathetic editing and picture research. For permission to reproduce Margaret Bennett's photographs, thanks to Margaret Bennett herself and to the School of Scottish Studies Archives at the University of Edinburgh. As always, I am grateful to the staff of the National Library of Scotland, especially Kevin Halliwell.

Thank you, too, to Arthur Blue, for his railway expertise, walking the dog and much else.

Jenni Calder

Index

Fraserburgh Society. *See* Aberdeen, Banff and
  Kincardineshire Society
Fraser's Highlanders, 26, 33, 34, 39
French and Indian Wars, 4, 45, 47, 157
fur trade *See* Hudson's Bay Company; North
West Company

Galbraith, JK, 52, 65–7
Galbraiths, 66
Galloway, 36
Galt, 56, 158
Galt, Alexander, 119
Galt, John, 12, 22, 50, 56–60, 62, 63, 90, 119
Gaspé Peninsula, 35
George III, 5, 36, 47
Germany, 3
Gillis, Ann, 51, 146
Gillis, Malcolm, 138
Gilmour, Allan, 40
Glace Bay, 44, 142, 150
Glace Bay Miners' Museum, The, 141–42
Glasgow, 3, 11, 16, 29, 37, 38, 43, 48, 80,
  104, 105, 106, 120, 134, 147, 152, 161
Glasgow Colonial Society, 159
Glasgow Journal, 5, 8, 27, 38
Glenaladale, 27, 29
Glenbow Museum, 162
Glencoe, 97, 127
Glencoe, Ontario, 66
Glen Dochart, 76
Glenelg, 42, 104
Glengarry, 47, 48, 116, 139
Glengarry County, 47, 48, 49, 50, 51, 87, 96,
  146, 149
Glengarry Fencibles, 48
Glengarry Pioneer Museum, 162
Glengarry School Days, 51, 147
Glen Lyon, 77
Glenlyon Peak, 77
Glennie, Thomas, 109
Glenshee, 114
Globe (Toronto), 116, 117, 159
Goderich, 61
gold, 107–09, 119, 160
Gordon, John, of Cluny, 14, 129, 159
Gordon, Sir Robert, 24, 157
Gows, 66
Grahams, 66
Grand Portage, 69, 71
Grande Prairie, 149
Grangemouth, 40
Grant, Cuthbert sr, 99
Grant, Cuthbert jr, 99, 100, 102, 159

Grant, Rev George, 120, 122, 160
Grant, JM, 45, 46
Great Bear Lake, 137
Great Lakes, 38, 113, 122, 128
Great Slave Lake, 80, 99
Greenock, 1, 16, 21, 25, 26, 37, 42, 51, 53,
  113, 161
Greenock Advertiser, 55
Gregory, John, 72
Grosse Ile, 21, 159
Guelph, 12, 57, 61, 146, 159
Guelph Civic Museum, 162
Gulf of Mexico, 2
Gulf of St Lawrence, 20, 29, 40
Gunn, Robert, 98

Halifax, 22, 31, 32, 33, 37, 39, 42, 121,
  125, 131, 140, 157, 162
*Hand–book and Guide to Manitoba and the
North–west*, 16
Hargrave, James, 76, 79
Hargrave, Letitia, 76, 94, 108
Harris, 1, 16, 130, 138, 151, 161
Hastings County, 62
Hawick, 76, 79
Hayes River, 98
Hearne, Samuel, 74, 157
Hector Centre, Pictou, 162
Hector, James, 121, 126
Heights of Abraham, 34
High River, 149
Highland Clearances, 9, 10–11, 14, 15, 35, 96
Highland Folk Museum, 161
Highland games, 148–49
Highland Land League, 15, 129
Highland Settler, 138
Highland societies (Canada), 144, 145, 147, 149
Highland Society (London), 9, 145
Highland Village, Lake Bras D'Or, 162
Hill, James J, 122, 123
Hints to Emigrants, 12, 19
Historical and Scientific Society of Manitoba, 77
'Home and Away' exhibition, 154
Hope Mountains, 111
Howison, John, 48, 49, 50, 86–7
Hoy, 61
Hudson Bay, 38, 45, 70, 79, 97, 117
Hudson River, 38, 47
Hudson's Bay Company, 2, 37, 69–70, 73–9,
  81, 82, 83–6, 89, 90, 91, 94, 95, 97, 98,
  100, 101, 102, 103, 106, 107, 110, 111,
  112, 123, 126, 127, 133,144, 151, 155,
  157, 158, 159, 160, 161

Some other books published by **Luath Press**

Scots in the USA

Jenni Calder

ISBN 978-1-908373-38-0 PBK £9 .99

The map of the United States is
peppered with Scottish placenames and America's telephone
directories are filled with surnames
illustrating Scottish ancestry.
Increasingly, Americans of Scottish
extraction are visiting Scotland
in search of their family history.
All over Scotland and the United
States there are clues to the
Scottish–American relationship,
the legacy of centuries of trade and
communication as well as that of
departure and heritage.
The experiences of Scottish settlers
in the United States varied enormously, as did their attitudes to the
lifestyles that they left behind and those that they began anew once they
arrived in North America.

Scots in the USA discusses why they left Scotland, where they went once
they reached the United States, and what they did when they got there.

*A reminder of the days when Scots were inventors, entrepreneurs and
pioneers, by the time you turn the last page, if you're not Scottish you'll
want to be.* THE DAILY RECORD

Luath Press Limited

committed to publishing well written books worth reading

LUATH PRESS takes its name from Robert Burns, whose little collie Luath (*Gael.*, swift or nimble) tripped up Jean Armour at a wedding and gave him the chance to speak to the woman who was to be his wife and the abiding love of his life. Burns called one of the 'Twa Dogs' Luath after Cuchullin's hunting dog in Ossian's *Fingal*.
Luath Press was established in 1981 in the heart of Burns country, and is now based a few steps up the road from Burns' first lodgings on Edinburgh's Royal Mile. Luath offers you distinctive writing with a hint of unexpected pleasures.
Most bookshops in the UK, the US, Canada, Australia, New Zealand and parts of Europe, either carry our books in stock or can order them for you. To order direct from us, please send a £sterling cheque, postal order, international money order or your credit card details (number, address of cardholder and expiry date) to us at the address below. Please add post and packing as follows: UK – £1.00 per delivery address; overseas surface mail – £2.50 per delivery address; overseas airmail – £3.50 for the first book to each delivery address, plus £1.00 for each additional book by airmail to the same address. If your order is a gift, we will happily enclose your card or message at no extra charge.

Luath Press Limited
543/2 Castlehill
The Royal Mile
Edinburgh EH1 2ND
Scotland
Telephone: +44 (0)131 225 4326 (24 hours)
Fax: +44 (0)131 225 4324
email: sales@luath. co.uk
Website: www. luath.co.uk